I0560874

Command the Morning, Day and Night

PRAYER M. MADUEKE

PRAYER PUBLICATIONS
210 Dyckman St New York,
NY 10040 United States

ISBN: 979-8638770143

Published by Prayer Publications.
Printed in the United States of America.

4 Free Ebooks

In order to say a 'Thank You' for purchasing *Command the Morning, Day and Night*, I offer these books to you in appreciation. Click or type **madueke.com/free-gift** in your browser.

Message from the Author

I want to see you succeed, grow, and break free from negativity and obstacles. My hope is for you to thrive, unaffected by negative influences and challenging situations. Because of that, please permit me to introduce two courses that I believe passionately will help you:

1. To break the evil altars and powers of your father's house, The role of altars in the realm of existence is very key because altars are meeting places between the physical and the spiritual, between the visible and the invisible.

   Unless a man cuts off the evil flow from the power of his father's house, he will not fulfil his destiny. Click here to learn more about my course on how to tear down unholy altars and close the enemy's entryways into your life!

2. To help you seamlessly break iron-like problems, illness, delayed marriage, poverty, or any long-standing battle.

   Discover the transformative power of Christian fasting and prayer. Remember, Matthew 17:21 teaches us, *"But this kind of demon does not go out except by prayer and fasting."* Ready to overcome your struggles? Click here to learn more about this course.

Embrace the journey ahead with faith, for through prayer, fasting, and the dismantling of evil altars, you shall unlock the doors to spiritual liberation and divine breakthrough. May your path be illuminated by His grace as you walk towards a life free from bondage.

If you're seeing this from the physical copy, type the link: madueke.com/courses in your browser to view all the courses on my website.

Prayer Madueke
CHRISTIAN AUTHOR

Christian Counselling

We were created for a greater purpose than only survival and God wants us to live a full life.

If you need prayer or counselling, or if you have any other inquiries, please visit the counselling page on my website to know when I will be available for a phone call.

Click or type links.madueke.com/counselling in your browser.

Let's Connect on Youtube ▶

Join me on my YouTube channel, "Prayer M. Madueke," where I share powerful insights, guidance, and prayers for spiritual breakthroughs.

Subscribe today to unlock the secrets of the Kingdom and embrace an abundant life. Let's grow together!

Click or type links.madueke.com/youtube in your browser.

Table of Contents

Closed Heaven, Reason to Command

When an individual or group of people breaks God's commandments, their heavens close. God said that when one decides to disobey His Word, his or her heavens will be closed. Refusing to hear God's Word is the same as being disobedient to Him. Hearing the Word of God and deciding not to do anything equally is despising God.

God made known in the Scriptures that He will appoint terror, consumption and burning ague that consumes the eye over those who despise or disobey Him (*See* Leviticus 26:16). Disobedience to God's Word is the primary reason for sorrows of heart and profitless hard labours that have filled the world today. When a person's heaven is closed, his enemies eat from the fruits of his labour.

God can depart from such persons. Their enemies will defeat them even in minor battles. Enemies of such people are usually much and they always suffer from hatred and rejection. They become servants to their supposed servants. Such people fear easily over nothing and feelings of insecurity overwhelm them.

The punishment for refusing to obey God's Word and keep His commandments will be multiplied sevenfold (*See* Leviticus 26:18). Everything that will happen to disobedient people has been outlined and written down by God so that no one will have any excuse.

> '*And I will break the pride of your power; and I will make your heaven as iron, and your earth as brass: And your strength shall be spent in vain: for your land shall not yield her increase, neither shall the trees of the land yield their fruits*'(Leviticus 26:19-20).

If you think that your immense wealth and prosperity will shield you from God's judgment and ensure you enjoy eternal life, you are either deceived or deceiving yourself. It is only a matter of time and your pride and strength of prosperity will be broken. All that gives you the power and make you proud will be dealt with. If you are enjoying open-heaven as a sinner, it will not last. The strength of your power and prosperity will be broken and you will be left with nothing. The flow of financial successes and material wealth do not last for a long time. God promised to make heaven as iron and earth as brass for disobedient and rebellious people.

> '*And I will break the pride of your power; and I will make your heaven as iron, and your earth as brass.*' (Leviticus 26:19-20).

It is foolish to gather wealth and enjoy life on earth without obedience to God's commandments. God's Word declares that sooner or later, the works of your hands will no longer prosper, and your strength and efforts in life will become wastes (*See* Leviticus 26:20).

However, God may not take away your life immediately. He may even allow you to regain your strength for a while, but you will spend it in rain. When you operate under a closed heaven, every investment you make will yield nothing. Your heaven will be caged and become as hard as iron and your earth as brass. You will suddenly begin to face impossibilities and experience business failures. Witches and wizards will invade your hard work on earth and your children will be brought under satanic attacks.

Your life and anything you do on earth will come under manipulations and become exposed to satanic attacks. Pestilence, increased number of enemies and lack of good things will characterize your life. At some other times, the earth will be made as iron, while the heaven above as brass. A person whose heavens are closed needs an urgent visitation of God.

INDIVIDUAL HEAVEN

When someone's heaven is closed, he ends up performing below divine expectation and his or her destiny stands the risk of being aborted. Such a person will remain unavailable for God's reach at all times.

> *And thy heaven that is over thy head shall be brass, and the earth that is under thee shall be iron (Deuteronomy 28:23).*

> *Oh, that thou wouldest rend the heavens, that thou wouldest come down, that the mountains might flow down at thy presence, (Isaiah 64:1).*

When personal heaven of one of the criminals crucified alongside with Jesus was closed, he railed at Jesus instead of pleading for mercy. He drew near to the saviour of the whole universe, yet he went to hellfire from the cross. If your heaven is closed, you may die in your bondage while people in the same bondage get delivered.

'And there were also two other, malefactors, led with him to be put to death... And one of the malefactors which were hanged railed on him, saying, if thou be Christ, save thyself and us' (Luke 23:32, 39).

When your heaven is closed, problems will always single you out amid others and deal with you.

'So, he went with them. And when they came to Jordan, they cut down wood but as one was felling a beam, the axe head fell into the water: and he cried, and said, Alas, master! for it was borrowed' (2 Kings 6:4-5).

Elijah and all the sons of the prophets were once cutting down woods near river Jordan. One of the sons of the prophets was marked out for his heaven was closed. Others were cutting down woods successfully, but the iron head of this particular man's axe fell into the river.

If your heaven is closed, others may succeed while you alone fail. Even with most envied academic certificates, you may make nothing meaningful out of them if your heaven is closed. As a beautiful young lady with a very good character, you may never be married once the heavens over your marriage are closed. Otherwise, you end up being married wrongly or to a wrong person and suffer for your entire life.

When your heaven is closed, death can single you out of a group of people even when it is not yet time for you to die. It would not matter whether you sit at the passenger's seat or the back seat. Death can by-pass others to locate you wherever you are sitting and take you.

When your heaven is closed, people can easily reject and hate you. They would rather favour others who cannot be compared as your equal. When your marital heaven is closed, your younger ones will all get married before you and even when you do, you will still fail in your marriage.

You can be easily exposed to accidents, premature death, poverty, failures, infirmities, destruction, business failures, periodical problems, backwardness, limitations and disappearance of riches when your heaven is closed. Good things will get away from you mysteriously beyond any logical explanation. You can experience strange occurrences, frustration, demotion, non-achievements, re-occurrence of similar problems and invisible barriers.

Having one's heaven closed makes one live a life of struggle, disappointments and disaster. Experiencing closed doors and making wrong choices are not uncommon with close heaven. When your heaven is closed, every effort you put becomes a waste and easy thing become too difficult for you to achieve. You can be confronted by evil yokes of bad habits, delay to progress and huge debts.

You will become tired of life, sooner or later, if you choose to do nothing urgently. Thoughts of suicide can begin to form the peak of your frustration. It is a dreaded experience to live life under closed heaven as it could result in one hating himself (or herself), finding costly faults in others and even cursing God.

Experiencing closed heaven is not peculiar to certain powerful personalities for it is not a respecter of persons or status. It does not respect where you come from. When Naaman's heaven was closed, he became a lonely leper amid his people. Though he was a captain, great, honourable, mighty man of valour and a national deliverance minister, he was a leper.

'Now Naaman, captain of the host of the king of Syria, was a great man with his master, and honorable, because by him the Lord had given deliverance unto Syria: he was also a mighty man in velour, but he was a leper' (2 Kings 5:1).

No matter your level in life or your class in society, if your heaven gets closed, you will be disgraced sooner or later. Your hands may look nice and clean but when your heaven is closed, whatever such hands touch will not prosper. Anything you lay your hands to do will have problems (*See* Matthew 12:10-31).

I know of a young boy that was born to a particular family. He later became the only child among other children that was always falling sick. It turned out that the heaven over his health was closed. The heaven over a particular area of a person's life can be closed up against the person. Under such circumstance, the person can become successful in every other area but not in that particular area of his life where his heaven is closed against him or her.

'*And when they were come to the multitude, there came to him a certain man, kneeling down to him, and saying, Lord, have mercy on my son: for he is lunatic, and sore vexed: for ofttimes he falleth into the fire, and oft into the water. And I brought him to thy disciples, and they could not cure him. Then Jesus answered and said, O faithless and perverse generation, how long shall I be with you? how long shall I suffer you? bring him hither to me. And Jesus rebuked the devil;*

and he departed out of him: and the child was cured from that very hour' (Matthew 17:14-18).

The heaven over the boy's health as mentioned in the Scripture above was closed up and he was fiercely tormented. He could have been the most intelligent and destined to take his family to the top. However, his heaven was closed up against him and he suffered endlessly nearing premature death. His father described him as a lunatic, sore vexed and often fell into fire or water.

It is a brutal experience to go through a closed heaven experience. It can make you feel rejected and abandoned by God and man. You can find it difficult to understand yourself. It can ruin your relationship with God. Life can become boring to you that you would wish you were dead.

Going through closed heaven experience may result in one discovering destiny and not being able to fulfil it. Closed heaven experience has cut short great destinies that were designed to have a massive impact on the earth. Victims of closed heavens are usually afflicted and oppressed right from birth even unto the grave. It has wasted many promising stars and has captured and destroyed great talents about to make international landmarks.

Closed heaven experience can abort a divine project or program of its victims and disgrace them out of this world without negotiations. It can kill and bury greatly destined individuals. It can elevate its victims and at the same time bring them down to shame and public disgrace and then close up every good door of opportunities. It can cause its victims to abandon good things halfway or at the edge of completion.

It can keep people away from God's plan and purpose, and manipulate them to go to the wrong places and meet wrong people or hand them over to their worst enemies on earth. It can lead you to the wrong partner, reduce God's grace upon your life, attack its victims with demonic fears and destroy their professions. It can remove hopes of her victims and place a curse upon them or yoke their lives with impossibilities.

Personal closed heaven is worse than other forms of closed heavens. In its working, it isolates you before dealing with you alone. It is capable of making a wise person look foolish in the eyes of his or her colleagues, and even among fools. It can reduce a person to nothing and put those who are destined to succeed in the class of defeated ones.

Most of its victims leave this world in pain, regrets, heartbreaks, deep tears and without helpers. They suffer without knowing the reasons behind their travails. Their divine helpers are most times dealt with ruthlessly or are pushed far off from them to disable from offering any help to the victims of personal closed heaven.

Though some victims may have all that it takes to succeed, they will never be allowed to succeed. The entire creation will abandon them at the time of their needs. Other people with bigger problems can get help easily but victims of personal closed heaven suffer without help. They suffer lack amid plenty and die in agony and want of all things.

'*And when the child was grown, it fell on a day, that he went out to his father to the reapers. And he said unto his father, My head, my head. And he said to a lad, Carry him to his mother. And when he had taken him, and brought him to his mother, he sat on her knees till noon, and then died*' (2 Kings 4:18-20).

Often, it may allow you to grow up a business, or get the best certificates or job, but it will not allow you to be alive to enjoy the fruits of your efforts. At the time of need, nobody can be able to help you unless God. Evil powers in charge of personally closed doors are wicked and heartless.

CLOSED FAMILY HEAVEN

'And will make thine house like the house of Jeroboam the son of Nebat, and like the house of Baasha the son of Ahijah, for the provocation wherewith thou hast provoked me to anger (1 Kings 21:22).

Some personally closed heavens have their roots in the foundation of the family. In most cases, what a person does in his or her life lives on even after death. Ahab's action against Naboth affected his entire household.

> *'And it came to pass, when Ahab heard that Naboth was dead, that Ahab rose up to go down to the vineyard of Naboth the Jezreelite, to take possession of it.... Behold, I will bring evil upon thee, and will take away thy posterity, and will cut off from Ahab him that pisseth against the wall, and him that is shut up and left in Israel, And will make thine house like the house of Jeroboam the son of Nebat, and like the house of Baasha the son of Ahijah, for the provocation*

wherewith thou hast provoked me to anger, and made Israel to sin. And of Jezebel also spake the Lord, saying, the dogs shall eat Jezebel by the wall of Jezreel. Him that dieth of Ahab in the city the dogs shall eat; and him that dieth in the field shall the fowls of the air eat (1 Kings 21:16-24).

It did not only close Ahab's heavens but it also affected everyone born into his family. When a family's heaven is closed, evil spirits take over, and the family's posterity is taken away so that untimely death reigns over every member of that particular family. The consequences of closed heaven over a family are much.

'*And when Jehu was come to Jezreel, Jezebel heard of it; and she painted her face, and tired her head, and looked out at a window. And as Jehu entered in at the gate, she said, Had Zimri peace, who slew his master? And he lifted up his face to the window, and said, who is on my side? who? And there looked out to him two or three eunuchs. And he said, Throw her down. So, they threw her down: and some of her blood was sprinkled on the wall, and on the horses: and he trode her under foot. And when he was come in, he did eat and drink, and said, Go, see now this cursed woman, and bury her: for she is a king's daughter. And they went to bury her: but they found no more of her than the skull, and the feet, and the palms of her hands. Wherefore they came again, and told him. And he said, This is the word of the Lord, which he spake by his servant Elijah the Tishbite, saying, In the portion of Jezreel shall dogs eat the flesh of Jezebel: And the carcase of Jezebel shall be as dung upon the face of the field in the portion of Jezreel; so that they shall not say, This is Jezebel* (2 Kings 9:30-37).

When the heaven of an individual or a group of people is closed, the number of their enemies will multiply. All manner of problems set in including possible mass death, disgrace, insults and reproaches. It can breed desires to shed blood and number of curses permitted to operate will increase. There will be a denial of rights, benefits and entitlements and disregard to authority.

'*And Ahab had seventy sons in Samaria. And Jehu wrote letters, and sent to Samaria, unto the rulers of Jezreel, to the elders, and to them that brought up Ahab's children, saying.... Then he wrote a letter the second time to them, saying, if ye be mine, and if ye will hearken unto my voice, take ye the heads of the men your master's sons, and come to me to Jezreel by tomorrow this time. Now the king's sons, being seventy persons, were with the great men of the city, which brought them up. And it came to pass, when the letter came to them, that they took the king's sons, and slew seventy persons, and put their heads in baskets, and sent him them to Jezreel. And there came a messenger, and told him, saying, they have brought the heads of the king's sons. And he said, Lay ye them in two heaps at the entering in of the gate until the morning* (2 Kings 10:1, 6-8).

When the heavens over Ahab's family got closed, they became deficient spiritually. The effects of closed heavens manifested physically in Ahab's family for more than three years. The first experience was when Ahab went to war, he was defeated and killed. Later, his wife, Jezebel, was despised, intimidated and thrown down from the window of her house. Her blood splashed on the wall and horses and was trodden under feet. She was eaten up by dogs leaving only her skull, feet and palms.

The seventy sons of Ahab in Samaria were not spared. They were killed and their heads were gathered in baskets and sent to

Jezreel. They were laid in two heaps at the entrance of the city gate until the next morning. The family closed heaven affected the whole house of Ahab in Jezreel, his great men, king-folks and his priests.

'Know now that there shall fall unto the earth nothing of the word of the Lord, which the Lord spake concerning the house of Ahab: for the Lord hath done that which he spake by his servant Elijah. So, Jehu slew all that remained of the house of Ahab in Jezreel, and all his great men, and his kinsfolks, and his priests, until he left him none remaining' (2 King 10:10-11).

When a family's heaven is closed, disaster takes over and good things run away. The heaven over an individual, family, group, tribe, race or nation can be closed. When heaven is closed globally, recession, insecurity becomes the order of the day. When the heavens over a nation are closed, there will be national crises and all manner of problems will emerge (*See* Daniel 10:12-17, Jeremiah 25: 11-15).

When the heavens over the children of Israel were closed, they suffered defeat and were captured for seventy years. Within those years of closed heaven, they suffered in hands of their enemies. Their cities were burnt and the walls of the temple broken down. They went into slavery for seventy years. Their main cities were made desolate and solitary. The inhabitants went sore and their tears ran down their cheeks. Their comfort was taken away. They were betrayed by treacherous friends and were ruthlessly dealt with.

Israel went into captivity under a family closed heaven. They were greatly afflicted and made slaves among the heathen. They no longer had rest. They were persecuted and all their good days of feasting were aborted. Their adversaries became their chief slave masters and their young girls were deflowered by strangers. Their wealth was coveted by their enemies. Their beauty departed and their princes found no pastures. Their misery increased in the hands of their enemies. They were mocked, dishonoured, trodden under feet and swallowed up. All their inheritance went to strangers (*See* Lamentation 5:1-22).

They were made orphans and widows. They suffered inhumanly and laboured for their enemies to enjoy an easy life. They were abandoned by God for seventy years because of their sins. Their heaven was closed up and their prayers could not reach the throne of God. The anger of the Lord was kindled against them. The temple of God was invaded by enemies, evil militants and herdsmen. The Levites, leaders and ministers were murdered without help. The house of God was burnt down completely and no pillar was left standing in the land. Congregational prayers and the prayers of corrupt elders failed except the neglected few believers, the young Daniel.

> '*They have cast fire into thy sanctuary, they have defiled by casting down the dwelling place of thy name to the ground. They said in their hearts, let us destroy them together: they have burned up all the synagogues of God in the land*' (Psalms 74:7-8).

Daniel began to pray and his prayers got breakthrough after seventy years. His prayers opened up the heaven that was closed over the nation of Israel.

> '*Then said he unto me, Fear not, Daniel: for from the first day that thou didst set thine heart to understand, and to chasten thyself before thy God, thy words were heard, and I am come for thy words. But the prince of the kingdom of Persia withstood me one and twenty days: but, lo, Michael, one of the chief princes, came to help me; and I remained there with the kings of Persia*' (Daniel 10:12-13).

When an angel from God was coming down to bring answers to Daniel's request, there was a blockage in the heavenlies. The powers in the heavenlies refused to let the angel of God pass through the heavens that were closed over the nation. For seventy years, no petition was honoured. A serious argument busted in the heavenlies for good twenty-one days, that God had to send reinforcement to challenge the host of darkness blocking the heavens over the children of Israel.

When the angel finally came to Daniel, he revealed to him that his prayers were answered right from the first day he started to pray but that there was a closed heaven over the nation. Some princes stand behind every closed heaven to ensure that all blessings coming from God do not reach its victims here on earth. If at any point, the person praying insists on receiving answers, their heaven will open. Closed heavens can be compared to a stronghold.

'*For though we walk in the flesh, we do not war after the flesh: (For the weapons of our warfare are not carnal, but mighty through God to the pulling down of strong holds)*' (2 Corinthians 10:3-4).

Rome was the world superpower in the days of Jesus Christ and Paul. Emperor Caesar had representatives all over the world who gather the best of things out of each nation and send them to Rome. The Romans enjoyed the best the world could offer. However, they began to lack in supplies of all their craving, which was regularly sent to them by these representatives all over the nations. It was later discovered, after research that a strongman has taken over the sea to loot all supplies going to Rome. Pirates and international robbers on the high sea built a stronghold on the sea to rob Romans of their supplies from all nations.

The problem persisted until the emperor complained of lack of supplies from their Roman representatives who insisted on their part, they had not failed in sending constant supplies to Rome. However, when the stronghold was later uncovered, Rome discovered that she does not possess any equipment capable of destroying the pirates. The stronghold was so fortified and rooted in the depth of the sea.

Under the frustration, the emperor summoned his military generals and mandated them to destroy the pirate's stronghold. In the Roman law at that time, failure to meet up with a mandated assignment warrant a death penalty. But before the actual death, failed victims are subjected to tortures that are worse than death. So, what the victims did always was to commit suicide instead of going through torture.

The military leader at that time who had received so much salary and other benefits for long years from the government sensed trouble. To him, it was a matter of life and death. However, he left with his soldiers without the strong military capability to compare with the strength of the stronghold. That was when the military was militant, not by struggling with an innocent group of civilians in Umuahia with sticks and avoiding the real terrorist group up north.

Under frustration, he set off with his trained soldiers to fight against their enemy's stronghold. Their first battle was to engage in a war with pirates and robbers on the high sea. He successfully defeated Rome's enemy and chased them out of their stronghold. Convincingly, strongholds built against Rome collapsed. That was how the Romans began to enjoy abundant supplies again. They received an uninterrupted flow of all manner of goods like gold and silver coming into their cities from all the nations.

` Paul, a historian and scholar, and a former Roman citizen knew the history. By the time he wrote to the church at Corinth the second time, he told them about spiritual stronghold. During the time of the Roman Empire, it was a physical stronghold. But at the time of the Corinthian church, it was a spiritual stronghold or what we call closed heaven. Paul told them of the battle to fight, which was not carnal like in the time of the Roman government. He told them of spiritual blockages and closed heavens. He informed them of spiritual armed robbers blocking their heavens.

> '*For though we walk in the flesh, we do not war after the flesh: (For the weapons of our warfare are not carnal, but mighty through God to the pulling down of strong holds;) Casting down imaginations, and every high thing that exalteth itself against the knowledge of God, and bringing into captivity every thought to the obedience of Christ* (2 Corinthians 10:3-5).

The church at Corinthian was highly prayerful, making all their requests known to God, but they were not receiving the answers to their prayers. They maintained a good relationship with God and certain their names were written in the book of life, but they were going through lots of challenges at that time. Some of them that prayed for marriages were already at their old ages. Frustrations characterized the lives of many others who were very poor, sick and were going through lots of impossibilities.

When Paul heard of their conditions and started praying for them, God opened his eyes and he saw a stronghold built against the Corinthian church in the heavenlies. He saw that all the things they needed and had been praying for were sent to them from heaven but spiritual armed robbers choked their heavens and denied them of all their blessings. They had been praying all kinds of prayers, asking, seeking and knocking but answers to their prayers never came to them (*See* Daniel 10:12-13).

What they needed was to move a little forward in prayers of persistence. They needed to move from praying carnally to spiritual prayers. They needed to look beyond their problems and frustrations. They needed to unite and see themselves as brethren. They needed to see the spirit of love for one another transcend spirit of division in the church.

> '*For ye are yet carnal: for whereas there is among you envying, and strife, and divisions, are ye not carnal, and walk as men? For while one saith, I am of Paul; and another, I am of Apollos; are ye not carnal?* (1 Corinthians 3:3-4).

Paul discovered that their problems were more spiritual than carnal. If they had to succeed, they were to do so through God alone and not by joining evil groups, receiving monetary favours, bribes and getting witchcraft powers. They had to grow mightily in God and not by fighting themselves. Paul told them that they have to be spiritual to pull down their stronghold and open their closed heavens with spiritual weapons. They had to deal with all evil in the hearts, cutting down evil imaginations and doing away with anything that opposes Christ's way of life and unity.

Christ must have to be given the chance to rule and reign in every area of their lives. They had to love each other and be united to fight a common enemy, the devil. To fight well, a new set of rules had to be set across church boundaries. They have to put on military uniforms ready to kill in the battle in the time of judgment.

'*To everything there is a season, and a time to every purpose under the heaven*' (Ecclesiastes. 3:1).

You have to put off civilian nature to pull down strongholds or open closed heavens. It is worse to face spiritual armed robbers than physical armed robbers.

'*The Lord hath opened his armory, and hath brought forth the weapons of his indignation: for this is the work of the Lord God of hosts in the land of the Chaldeans. Come against her from the utmost border, open her storehouses: cast her up as heaps, and destroy her utterly: let nothing of her be left. Slay all her bullocks; let them go down to the slaughter: woe unto them! for their day is come, the time of their visitation'* (Jeremiah 50:25-27).

Spiritual forces in charge of strongholds and closed heavens are very experienced in spiritual warfare. God does not fight them with ordinary weapons. Our God has provided us with His entire armoury for us to use right weapons of warfare to open up satanic warehouses and storerooms to set all the oppressed free. You need to put on the whole armour, including judgmental uniform and all holiness to be able to stand against every evil.

'Finally, my brethren, be strong in the Lord, and in the power of his might. Put on the whole armor of God that ye may be able to stand against the wiles of the devil. For we wrestle not against flesh and blood, but against principalities, against powers, against the rulers of the darkness of this world, against spiritual wickedness in high places. Wherefore take unto you the whole armor of God, that ye may be able to withstand in the evil day, and having done all, to stand' (Ephesians 6:10-13).

A fight to open closed heavens or pull-down stronghold is not a fight for ordinary civilians elders or youths who only knows one style of warfare strategically. Tailors, ordinary security agents and inexperienced civilians do not engage in this kind of battles. They are meant for militants who are trained to kill in a split of second with spiritual missiles those who are appointed to die under their oath of the covenant with death. It is also not meant for carnal, or immoral and undisciplined soldiers who sleep overnight with the loose Delilahs and Jezebels.

'*And she said, The Philistines be upon thee, Samson. And he awoke out of his sleep, and said, I will go out as at other times before, and shake myself. And he wist not that the Lord was departed from him*' (Judges 16:20).

The battle to open up closed heavens or pull-down strongholds is meant for matured soldiers who are saved. These are children of God who are also zealous and self-denying soldiers of Jesus Christ, clothed with humility, wise as serpents, harmless as a dove, strong in faith, and are not staggering at the promises of God. They are approved soldiers who can kill and bury demons and their vowed agents under evil oath to destroy without mercy through spiritual warfare.

> *And when it was day, certain of the Jews banded together, and bound themselves under a curse, saying that they would neither eat nor drink till they had killed Paul. And they were more than forty which had made this conspiracy. And they came to the chief priests and elders, and said, we have bound ourselves under a great curse, that we will eat nothing until we have slain Paul (Acts 23:12-14).*

> *And Moses was very wroth, and said unto the Lord, Respect not thou their offering: I have not taken one ass from them, neither have I hurt one of them... And there came out a fire from the Lord, and consumed the two hundred and fifty men that offered incense (Numbers 16:15, 35).*

This kind of warfare cannot be fought by lazy, selfish, careless, indifferent worldly soldiers who cannot discern the time. Spiritually warfare is for soldiers who can fight all day and all nights until the last enemy is dead. They are trained for victory and principled for the life of spiritual fitness to contend to the end. They are always ready to enter into any strong man's house to recover all the ancient losses.

'Lift up your heads, O ye gates; and be ye lift up, ye everlasting doors; and the King of glory shall come in. Who is this King of glory? The Lord strong and mighty, the Lord mighty in battle. Lift up your heads, O ye gates; even lift them up, ye everlasting doors; and the King of glory shall come in' (Psalms 24:7-9).

Determined soldiers on a mission to open their closed heavens must be angry without mercy against all evil forces opposed to their lives moving forward. They must be spiritually certified militants, vibrant and ready to pray *'bulldozing prayers'* that can penetrate every dark room to recover every loss. Every spiritual checkpoint must be overtaken. Satanic warehouses must be invaded and emptied.

Warfare soldiers must dismantle all evil bumps of unprofitable delays. Arrested businesses, true worships, great talents and projects must be released. Soldiers that must open the closed heavens and pulled down strongholds, command the morning, day and night must:

- Separate from sin
- Submit to the authority of Scriptures
- Pray in the name of Jesus
- Practice self-denial, not self-indulgence and separate from evil covenants.

2

Separation from Sin

M ajority of churchgoers, so-called believers in Christian leaderships of our time who COMMAND the morning are not separated from sin. Sin is a rebellion against God and His Word. Therefore, you must keep a great distance from sin and evil in all its forms to be able to open up closed heavens or pull-down strongholds.

'Let him that stole steal no more: but rather let him labor, working with his hands the thing which is good, that he may have to give to him that needeth. Let no corrupt communication proceed out of your mouth, but that which is good to the use of edifying, that it may minister grace unto the hearers. And grieve not the

Holy Spirit of God, whereby ye are sealed unto the day of redemption. Let all bitterness, and wrath, and anger, and clamor, and evil speaking, be put away from you, with all malice' (Ephesians 4:28-31).

You may have been the worst sinner who is very unclean and defiled, but you can repent and ask God for forgiveness, as you determine to stay away from sin and start doing what is good. You must do away with corruption, honour the Holy Spirit, avoid all bitterness of heart and put away malice. You must learn to move closer to Jesus and fellow true believers to grow in faith.

'Abide in me, and I in you. As the branch cannot bear fruit of itself, except it abide in the vine; no more can ye, except ye abide in me. I am the vine, ye are the branches: He that abideth in me, and I in him, the same bringeth forth much fruit: for without me ye can do nothing' (John 15:4-5).

'Not forsaking the assembling of ourselves together, as the manner of some is; but exhorting one another: and so much the more, as ye see the day approaching' (Hebrews 10:25).

The consequences of sin are many. They can separate you from God and godly helpers, and place curses upon your life. Sin can close someone's heaven; short-change the person's destiny making him or her fugitive and vagabond. It can close your heaven and make you a servant of your servants. It can bring confusion into your life, scattering your united family and terminate all your projects.

Sin can close your heaven, and build strongholds to keep your husband, children or wife far away from within your reach. It can close people's heavens and imprison them with evil characters making them be despised and bringing fears into their hearts. The sin of disobedience made Lot's wife become a pillar of salt after closing up her heaven separating her from God for eternity. Sin can cause spiritual blindness and attack you with all manner of curses and rob all your blessings.

Sin can close people's heavens and deprive them of comfort, riches, honour and great wealth. It can torment you with grave feelings of guilt or condemnation and trouble you unto death. Sin can give birth to many problems, cause delays, hinder deliverances, keep people in bondage, bring insecurity, denial of true worship and swallow people's destinies. It can take people out of divine coverage and waste people's lifetime efforts.

Sin can make a mockery of a well-respected person and make him a laughing stock. It can build an evil wall against you shutting you out of God's program and plans. It can deliver someone to his or her enemies to be tormented to death with no moment of rest. It can judge, condemn and kill without negotiations. It can bring defeat, destruction, and denial of rights, benefits and entitlements. Sin can paralyze and make anyone impotent.

Afterward Jesus findeth him in the temple, and said unto him, Behold, thou art made whole: sin no more, lest a worse thing come unto thee (John 5:14).

I must work the works of him that sent me, while it is day: the night cometh, when no man can work (John 9:4).

Whenever Jesus delivers a person, His counsel is always, '*Go and sin no more lest a worse thing come upon thee*'. When Saul, the first king of Israel, sinned against God by offering the wrong sacrifice, his situation became worse and God took away his kingdom and gave it another. He sought help from a witch and died in disgrace.

David committed immorality and sword dwelled in his household. Evil was raised against him and his family and many lives were wasted as a result of death. Sin has never made anyone's life or destiny better irrespective of pleasures it offers at the beginning. Christ's counsel is for us to separate ourselves from sin.

'*She said, No man, Lord. And Jesus said unto her, neither do I condemn thee: go, and sin no more*' (John 8:11).

'*Be ye not unequally yoked together with unbelievers: for what fellowship hath righteousness with unrighteousness? and what communion hath light with darkness? And what concord hath Christ with Belial? or what part hath he that believeth with an infidel? And what agreement hath the temple of God with idols? for ye are the temple of the living God; as God hath said, I will dwell in them, and walk in them; and I will be their God, and they shall be my people. Wherefore come out from among them, and be ye separate, saith the Lord, and touch not the unclean thing; and I will receive you, and will be a Father unto you, and ye shall be my sons and daughters, saith the Lord Almighty*' (2 Corinthians 6:14-18).

Sin banished Absalom out of his comfort zone for three years and later got him killed him. Sin disgraced King Asa and later ate up his feet unto death.

> 'But the high places were not removed: nevertheless, Asa's heart was perfect with the Lord all his days... The rest of all the acts of Asa, and all his might, and all that he did, and the cities which he built, are they not written in the book of the Chronicles of the kings of Judah? Nevertheless, in the time of his old age he was diseased in his feet' (1 king 15:14, 23).

Sin disappointed Judas Iscariot, disgraced and forced him to commit suicide. It can make people foolish, blind and evilly end their lives. You have to do away with sin and all satanic properties to open your heavens, pull down strongholds and live life in abundance being separated from the devil.

> 'And many that believed came, and confessed, and shewed their deeds. Many of them also which used curious arts brought their books together, and burned

them before all men: and they counted the price of them, and found it fifty thousand pieces of silver' (<u>Acts 19:18-19</u>).

You cannot serve two masters at the same time. You need Jesus Christ. Likewise, you need to separate yourself from sin. You need to be born again. Having recognized you have sinned and ran short of God's glory, confess your sins and turn away from them permanently. Your decision must be genuine and sincere. You must turn from all your evil thoughts and sinful desires.

When you entrust your heart to Jesus and ask Him to control all your life, your life desires and movements of thoughts would change. You will begin to develop hatred for sin, desiring for a love relationship with God more than anything else. Someone who is separated from sin brings evil and every other rebellion against God to an absolute end. There is no short cut to open your closed heaven and pull-down strongholds other than separating from sin. When you try to pull down stronghold or open your closed heaven without separation from sin, worse things will likely come upon you. It will be the worst deceit to let anyone convince you that you can enjoy open-heaven on earth and pull-down strongholds while leaving in sin.

'There was a certain rich man, which was clothed in purple and fine linen, and fared sumptuously every day: ... And it came to pass, that the beggar died, and was carried by the angels into Abraham's bosom: the rich man also died, and was buried; And in hell he lift up his eyes, being in torments, and seeth Abraham afar off, and Lazarus in his bosom. And he cried and said, Father Abraham, have mercy on me, and send Lazarus, that he may dip the tip of his finger in water, and cool my tongue; for I am tormented in this flame. But Abraham said, Son, remember that thou in thy lifetime receivedst thy good things, and likewise Lazarus evil things: but now he is comforted, and thou art tormented' (Luke 16:19, 22-25).

The height of ignorance and deceit is to believe you can get an open-heaven, defeat a determined enemy without separation from sin. God cannot be deceived; whatever a man sows is what he will surely reap. Separation from sin is a prerequisite to open-heaven and true enjoyment of life on earth. To pull down strongholds and yet remain in the bondage of sin is pure deceit and ending up in eternal torment of hell will cause sinners to forget all past enjoyment sin offered them.

OBEDIENCE TO SCRIPTURES

In all preaching, teachings and ministration of God's Word, God views obedience as the most important aspect to all. Submission to the Scriptures, which is the practical aspect of loving God, must be our major goal. This is what most people who encourage you to command the morning, day and night will not tell you.

> '*But be ye doers of the word, and not hearers only, deceiving your own selves. For if any be a hearer of the word, and not a doer, he is like unto a man beholding his natural face in a glass: For he beholdeth himself, and goeth his way, and straightway forgetteth what manner of man he was. But whoso looketh into the perfect law of liberty, and continueth therein, he being not a forgetful hearer, but a doer of the work, this man shall be blessed in his deed*' (James 1:22-25).

If you love God, then you have to fall in love with His Word and obey it. You must labour to maintain uninterrupted obedience to God's Word to command the morning and open your closed heaven. Any man or woman who does not have a genuine love for God cannot submit to the authority of Scriptures. There are millions of words, personalities, powers, within and around us contending to take supremacy over God's Word.

> '*Whom have I in heaven but thee? and there is none upon earth that I desire beside thee*' (Psalms 73:25).

> '*That I may know him, and the power of his resurrection, and the fellowship of his sufferings, being made conformable unto his death*' (Philippians 3:10).

You must, therefore, do everything possible to know and discern God's Word. You are expected to have an intense desire to know God more, and with all your strength oppose every other doctrine against God's Word. Such doctrines that do not submit to the authority of Scriptures must be seen as error and untrue.

> '*Make me to understand the way of thy precepts: so, shall I talk of thy wondrous works*' (Psalms 119:27).

> '*How sweet are thy words unto my taste! yea, sweeter than honey to my mouth!*' (Psalms 119:103).

'If any man will do his will, he shall know of the doctrine, whether it be of God, or whether I speak of myself' (John 7:17).

To command the morning, open your closed heaven and pull-down strongholds, you must have a purpose, establish a time to study to know God's Word and practice the whole truth. Lack of knowledge of God's Word may lead one into accepting what is wrong and can close someone's heaven. Paul's knowledge of Scriptures helped him pursue his ministry without minding his sufferings. He passed through grievous sufferings and went through painful hardships before his heavens were opened.

Understanding of Scriptures and putting them into practice leads to opened heaven irrespective of obstacles along the way. The fruit of obedience to God's Word opens closed heavens, pull down strongholds and cause believers to experience wondrous things. When you submit to God's Word, it opens closed heavens to establish the supremacy of God over all human needs.

'Then said Jesus unto them, when ye have lifted up the Son of man, then shall ye know that I am he, and that I do nothing of myself; but as my Father hath

taught me, I speak these things.... And ye shall know the truth, and the truth shall make you free (John 8:28, 32).

If you must experience open-heaven and enjoy God's blessings, you must live in obedience to the Word of God even at risks of death. Separation from sin and submission to the Scriptures are most potent and practical steps to attract open-heaven. Abel submitted to the Scriptures and God accepted his offerings and defended his soul. His heaven remained opened even after death and God fought his battles against his evil brother, Cain.

Enoch submitted to call of salvation and God opened his heaven and empowered him. He received favour to walk with God unto the day his heaven opened and received him alive. Noah obeyed God's Word, built an ark, lived righteously amid corrupt people and God opened his heavens. He received enough grace to live when others were dying under closed heavens. His submission to God's Word pulled down his strongholds.

Abraham submitted to God's instructions that called him out from the idolatrous foundation. When he obeyed, God opened his heaven, and pulled down all his strongholds and made his name great and a great nation came out of him. Through him, all nations and families of the earth were blessed. His seed multiplied as much as the dust of the earth. He was so much blessed until his curses were replaced with blessings from above. When his heaven opened, he became the father of many nations and kings emerged from his loins. He received an everlasting covenant and the land of Canaan was given to him for an everlasting possession.

God became God to him and his seeds, and Abraham possessed the gates of his enemies. When you endure all tests to obey God's Word, your heaven will surely open. Jacob obeyed and moved out of his father's house. He vowed to serve God, built a house for God and gave all his tithes and his heaven opened and remained open (*See* Genesis 29:1-22). God pulled down his strongholds, defended him before Laban, troubled all those that troubled him and changed his name from Jacob to Israel. Joseph submitted to God's Word and his heaven opened to interpret dreams. He was later made a manager in Potiphar's house, overseer in prisons and a prime minister in Egypt.

When your heaven is open and every stronghold pulled down, you can make it in life. No pharaoh, or any Egyptian army, evil herdsmen or their magicians can stand against anyone submissive to the Scriptures. When you submit to the authority of Holy Scriptures, your heaven will open, and your life will be divinely sponsored and empowered, making all your enemies surrender before you (Exodus 8:25-32, 9:29-35).

No one can succeed in pulling down a person whose heavens are open without bitter consequences. Miriam tried to overthrow Moses and she was attacked by leprosy. Cain killed Abel but became a vagabond and fugitive. The sons of Noah tried and they got confirmed until they scattered. The men of Sodom and Gomorrah tried to defile angels of God and they all became blind.

The Philistines tried to insult God and His people, Israel, but they lost Goliath and fell in battle. Laban tried it and God rebuked him. The Egyptian occultist, the magicians and their entertainment disappointed them. Ahithophel tried to advise Absalom against David, his father and king, but his counsel was turned into foolishness and he committed suicide. Shimei tried to curse David, but he was arrested and was later killed (2 Samuel 16:5-14, 19:16-23, 1 king 2:8-9, 36-46).

The king in Bethel tried it and his hand dried up. Ahab did evil in the sight of God and his family was wiped out of the earth in one day. Herod took God's glory and he was eaten up by worms alive. Bar-Jesus or Elymas tried to withstand Paul from winning a soul and he became blind (Acts 1:18-20).

Judas Iscariot betrayed his master, Jesus, and he went to hellfire straight after losing his ministry. It is not possible to despise the Scriptures or attack someone whose heaven is opened and go scot-free. To open your closed heaven and pull-down strongholds to enjoy steady opened heaven, you must separate yourself from sin and submit to the authority of Scriptures and pray in the name of Jesus. The Word of God is the final authority for all Christians. No man's education is complete without the knowledge of Scriptures. In George Washington's last address to the congress, he said 'It is impossible to rightly govern the world without God and the Bible. It is impossible to govern the universe without the aid of a supreme being'.

PRAYING WITH THE NAME OF JESUS

Open-heaven comes through prayers of faith. Prayer and faith must go together because prayer without faith is largely unprofitable. A great struggle lies ahead of every believer on earth, and it is only through prayers that one can overcome the devil. Many who have professed to be Christians have failed and fallen on days of battles due to lack of prayers. You are called to resist the devil through prayers. If you want answers every time you ask or command the morning you must follow godly principles and fulfil conditions necessary for answers to come.

'*Watch and pray, that ye enter not into temptation: the spirit indeed is willing, but the flesh is weak*' (Matthew 26:41).

'*And he spake a parable unto them to this end, that men ought always to pray, and not to faint*' (Luke 18:1).

Open-heaven comes through prayers of faith and we can only maintain it through prayers and thanksgiving. We must not pray like the heathen or hypocrites regarding iniquity in our hearts.

'And when ye stand praying, forgive, if ye have ought against any: that your Father also which is in heaven may forgive you your trespasses. But if ye do not forgive, neither will your Father which is in heaven forgive your trespasses' (Mark 11:25-26).

Prayer is an act of making our needs and desires known to God and waiting upon Him to answer. We fellowship with God through prayer, offering ourselves as living sacrifices, which are pleasing unto Him. You must not pray against God's revealed will in His written Word, or pray in unbelief. Fear, doubt, discouragement and unbelief are all negative substances that can work against the prayer of faith.

'Hast thou not known? hast thou not heard, that the everlasting God, the Lord, the Creator of the ends of the earth, fainteth not, neither is weary? there is no searching of his understanding. He giveth power to the faint; and to them that have no might he increaseth strength. Even the youths shall faint and be weary, and the young men shall utterly fall: But they that wait upon the Lord shall renew their strength; they shall

mount up with wings as eagles; they shall run, and not be weary; and they shall walk, and not faint (Isaiah 40:28-31).

A time of prayer is a time to commune with and wait on God. It is to be done at all times at any given opportunity. Praying in the name of Jesus is one of the most effective ways to receive immediate answers from God (*See* Philippians 2:9-11). God exalted Jesus highly and invested all powers upon Him, that all things can be made possible through the name of Jesus.

Jesus' name was placed above every other name, all things in heaven, earth and under earth bow at the mention of Jesus in prayers. No force of darkness can stop the working of Jesus' name. The name of Jesus can penetrate darkest kingdoms and rescue captives in times of prayer (*See* Proverbs 18:10). The name of Jesus Christ is the name of the Lord, and to be able to use that name and receive answers to all prayers, you must live righteously before God (*See* Psalms 66:18 20).

EFFICACY OF PRAYERS

- Noah prayed and his offerings to God were accepted, and the curse placed upon the earth was removed after the flood (*See* Genesis 7:7-13, 16-23).

- Abraham prayed for a child and God answered him at old age.

- Ishmael prayed and God heard him from heaven and sent help to him. God opened his mother's eyes and she saw a well of water.

- Isaac cried to God concerning his wife's bareness and her womb was opened.

- Jacob prayed and God heard him and later changed his name to Israel.

- The children of Israel prayed against the Egyptian bondage and God arose and broke their bondage.

- Moses cried unto God and the Red Sea blocking their way was parted into two.

- Joshua prayed and Achan was discovered. When he prayed again, the sun and the moon were suspended for a whole day.

- Jephthah prayed and God gave him victory over the children of Ammon.

- Samson prayed and God used him to bury the Philistines.

- Hanna prayed and God gave her a godly child called Samuel.

- David prayed and Goliath who rose against his nation, Israel, was defeated.

- Elijah prayed and heaven was shut for about three years.

- Elisha prayed and God gave him a double portion of Elijah's anointing.

- Hezekiah prayed and God extended his expired life to fifteen years more on earth.

- Jabez prayed against poverty and hardship and God promoted him and enlarged his coast.

- Jehoshaphat prayed and his enemies got confused and killed each other.

- Jeremiah prayed and God saved him and showed him great and mighty things which he knew not.

- Jonah prayed and God heard him and commanded the fish to vomit him by force.

- Daniel prayed and God shut mouths of lions assigned to waste his life.

- Esther prayed and the king's decree was changed.

- Nehemiah prayed and God moved the king to give him a national assignment.

- The thief on the cross prayed and Jesus answered and took him to heaven.

- Paul prayed and God opened his blinded eyes and commissioned him to preach.

- The apostle prayed at the Pentecost day and they were all baptized of the Holy Ghost and empowered for service.

- They prayed again and Aeneas who was sick received her healing.

- The apostles prayed and Dorcas who was dead was raised to life.

- Cornelius prayed and his entire household was saved.

- The church prayed and Peter was released from the prison.

Praying in the name of Jesus is the easiest way to receive answers to prayers. Heaven cannot remain closed when a true child of God prays in faith. No stronghold can stand against true prayers of a righteous man.

Carrying the Cross

There is a price to pay to effectively command the morning, the day, the night, open your heavens and keep it open. You don't just see a book like this and because there are prayers in it to command, you start commanding. Believing in Christ and accepting His doctrine is good, but there is needs to continue in obedience if you must maintain and enjoy open-heaven. You must continue in His Word to remain a true disciple indeed.

'Then said Jesus unto his disciples, if any man will come after me, let him deny himself, and take up his cross, and follow me. For whosoever will save his life shall lose it: and whosoever will lose his life for my sake shall find it. For what is a man profited, if he shall

gain the whole world, and lose his own soul? or what shall a man give in exchange for his soul? (Matthew 16:24-26).

For many Christians, the greatest hindrance to an open-heaven is the inability to deny *'self'*. Jesus said that if any man (of whatever rank or circumstance, or age or nation of the world) will "effectively" come after Him, let that man deny himself in all things and take up his cross of whatever kind and follow Him. Pitying your life when you are supposed to chasten it to obey God's Word is not self-denial.

Whatever is in your power to deny your body to get your heaven opened must not be avoided. The reason many people's heavens are not opened is that they lack discipline. The devil has successfully lured many people into complacency and ungodly things of this world to keep their heavens closed. Nobody can save his life by trading it to the devil in the name of survival. Eve entered into pleasure by eating the forbidden fruit and her heaven got closed. Balaam the prophet got greedy and went in for a life of covetousness. He loved money rather than obeying God's Word. His heaven got closed and he died with his sins. The children of Israel went into whoredom, ate things sacrificed to idols and many of them lost their lives. The presence of God departed from them and many of them died. (*See* Numbers 25:1-18).

Achan lacked self-control and took an accursed thing. He was stoned to death together with members of his family. His family's heaven closed forever. People who must command the morning and open their heaven, pull down their strongholds must live a life of self-denial and discipline.

'*But what things were gain to me, those I counted loss for Christ. Yea doubtless, and I count all things but loss for the excellency of the knowledge of Christ Jesus my Lord: for whom I have suffered the loss of all things, and do count them but dung, that I may win Christ, And be found in him, not having mine own righteousness, which is of the law, but that which is through the faith of Christ, the righteousness which is of God by faith: That I may know him, and the power of his resurrection, and the fellowship of his sufferings, being made conformable unto his death; If by any means I might attain unto the resurrection of the dead. Not as though I had already attained, either were already perfect: but I follow after, if that I may apprehend that for which also, I am apprehended of Christ Jesus. Brethren, I count not myself to have*

apprehended: but this one thing I do, forgetting those
things which are behind, and reaching forth unto those
things which are before, I press toward the mark for
the prize of the high calling of God in Christ Jesus'
(Philippians 3:7-14).

Paul denied himself an exalted position to open his heaven and
keep it open. He was circumcised on the eighth day in the tribe
of Benjamin and made a Hebrew of Hebrews. He was a very
zealous Pharisee and blameless in observing traditions and the
customs of this exalted people. He denied himself of this exalted
position to qualify to command his morning to obtain open-
heaven. He later joined Christians and became one of the
despised people as a result of belief in the gospel of Lord Jesus
Christ. He was severally beaten but he never stopped
proclaiming the gospel. He relinquished his highly exalted
position in society and settled with the commoners and the poor
brethren of the society.

'And after the uproar was ceased, Paul called unto him
the disciples, and embraced them, and departed for to
go into Macedonia. And when he had gone over those
parts, and had given them much exhortation, he came
into Greece, And there abode three months. And

when the Jews laid wait for him, as he was about to sail into Syria, he purposed to return through Macedonia. And there accompanied him into Asia Sopater of Berea; and of the Thessalonians, Aristarchus and Secundus; and Gaius of Derbe, and Timotheus; and of Asia, Tychicus and Trophimus. These going before tarried for us at Troas. And we sailed away from Philippi after the days of unleavened bread, and came unto them to Troas in five days; where we abode seven days' (Acts 20:1-6).

Paul was determined to preach in Jerusalem even if it means losing his life. Paul's key decisions in his life and self-denials helped him operate his ministry under open-heaven, fully determined to spread the gospel to many nations. He believed in total freedom, complete deliverance and constant open-heaven.

'I beseech you therefore, brethren, by the mercies of God, that ye present your bodies a living sacrifice, holy, acceptable unto God, which is your reasonable service. And be not conformed to this world: but be ye transformed by the renewing of your mind, that ye

may prove what is that good, and acceptable, and perfect, will of God (Romans 12:1-2).

His sacrifices and self-denials made him glory only in things that pertain to God. He determined not to build upon another man's foundation (*See* Romans 15:17-33). He sacrificed all things that did not glorify God, regardless of how beneficial they were to him personally. He denied himself many things to preach the gospel to all categories of people (*See* 1 Corinthians 1:1-16, 8:16-24, 11:9-33). He never engaged himself in anything that will close his heaven or hinder him from destroying works of the devil.

The sons of Eli engaged themselves in immorality and their heavens closed. That was why the family of Eli was rejected and they died shameful deaths. Solomon destroyed his kingdom when he engaged himself in immortality. He closed his heaven and that of many people in his house. Gehazi told a lie to receive tempting gifts and he closed his heaven and that of his children's generation.

The issue of close-heaven is not a simple matter for it can potentially affect unborn generations. Closed heaven causes war, destructions and mass deaths. A person with a closed heaven cannot pull down strongholds. When Goliath's heaven closed, he was messed up in a battle by a little and inexperienced boy,

David. When the heaven of the tribes of Dan closed, seventy thousand of them died under pestilence.

'And God was displeased with this thing; therefore, he smote Israel.... So, the Lord sent pestilence upon Israel: and there fell of Israel seventy thousand men. And God sent an angel unto Jerusalem to destroy it: and as he was destroying, the Lord beheld, and he repented him of the evil, and said to the angel that destroyed, it is enough, stay now thine hand. And the angel of the Lord stood by the threshing floor of Ornan the Jebusite. And David lifted up his eyes, and saw the angel of the Lord stand between the earth and the heaven, having a drawn sword in his hand stretched out over Jerusalem. Then David and the elders of Israel, who were clothed in sackcloth, fell upon their faces. And David said unto God, Is it not I that commanded the people to be numbered? even I it is that have sinned and done evil indeed; but as for these sheep, what have they done? let thine hand, I pray thee, O Lord my God, be on me, and on my father's house; but not on thy people, that they should be plagued' (1 Chronicles 21:7, 14 -17).

When Judas Iscariot's heaven closed, he abandoned his ministry and went for money that later became useless. The worst thing that can happen to anyone is to live under a closed heaven. But when your heaven is open, difficult things become easy and impossible things become possible. Peter's heaven opened and he became an employee automatically. When the heaven of one of the prophets' widow opened, she paid all her debts and opened an oil firm.

THE RESULT OF OPEN-HEAVEN

- Salvation and peace of mind
- Power in services to God and mankind
- Full redemption and healing
- All physical and spiritual provisions are available
- Evil spirits against marriages are frustrated easily
- Demons causing divorce in marriages are disgraced
- Separation in marriage becomes impossible
- Open-heaven heals bad relationships
- Open-heaven heals broken hearts
- Open-heaven removes troubles from marriage
- Married couples live in peace and harmony
- Open-heaven promotes the divine presence of God during courtship
- It brings joy and fulfilment in a honeymoon
- Open-heaven sustains the love of God in marriage
- Demons hindering conception is destroyed
- Open-heaven makes parents raise godly children
- Open-heaven destroys all sicknesses
- Open-heaven supplies people with divine strengths
- Open-heaven brings full restoration
- Open-heaven brings prosperity
- Open-heaven protects pregnant women
- Open-heaven destroys untimely death

- Open-heaven brings good health and true riches
- It helps people overcome office problems easily
- Open-heaven attracts good jobs for people
- Open-heaven delivers people from sexual problems
- Open-heaven makes people excel in all fields
- Open-heaven protects children, teenagers and youths from destruction
- It can prevent abortion and bring comfort to retain
- Open-heaven can deliver people from poverty
- Open-heaven can destroy unknown problems
- Open-heaven can enter into the heart and destroy heart diseases
- Open-heaven can give sound sleep
- Open-heaven can destroy bad habits
- Open-heaven can heal all manner of cancer
- Open-heaven can destroy demons
- Open-heaven can recover all the good things lost
- Open-heaven can stop witchcraft attacks
- Open-heaven can destroy incurable diseases
- Open-heaven can close evil doors
- Open-heaven can give comfort and safety
- Open-heaven can give confidence
- Open-heaven can bring financial successes
- Open-heaven can bring all manner of blessings and stop stress

PRAYING FOR OPEN-HEAVEN

1. Any principality in charge of the air against me, I command you be removed, in the name of Jesus.

2. Every door in the heavenlies blocking my way, I command you to be removed, in the name of Jesus.

3. Blood of Jesus, flow into the heavenlies and make a way for me, in the name of Jesus.

4. Any satanic wall standing against my life, collapse, in the name of Jesus.

5. Father Lord, open an account for me in the bank of heaven, in the name of Jesus.

6. Let every satanic store in the heavenlies release my blessings now, in the name of Jesus.

7. Holy Ghost fire, burn to ashes every satanic padlock, in the name of Jesus.

8. Let the anointing that breaks the yoke fall upon me, in the name of Jesus.

9. I command every satanic soldier raised against me to die, in the name of Jesus.

10. I bind and cast out every strongman against me in the heavenlies, in the name of Jesus.

11. Any evil delegate against my destiny, die, in the name of Jesus.

12. Let powers of every enemy against me in the heavenlies perish, in the name of Jesus.

13. O Lord, dispatch Your soldiers in the heavenlies for my sake, in the name of Jesus.

14. Let every demonic celestial and terrestrial powers against me die, in the name of Jesus.

15. Every satanic judgment passed against me in the heavenlies, be reversed, in the name of Jesus.

16. Any evil program against me in the heavenlies, be terminated, in the name of Jesus.

17. Any evil advancement against my life, scatter, in the name of Jesus.

18. I receive the divine mandate to prosper above my equals, in the name of Jesus.

19. I cut off every link between me and poverty, in the name of Jesus.

20. Every garment of reproach upon my life, catch fire, in the name of Jesus.

21. Every evil eye monitoring my life from the heavenlies, be blinded, in the name of Jesus.

22. Every enemy of my well-being in the heavenlies, die, in the name of Jesus.

23. Every curse working against my life in the heavenlies, expire, in the name of Jesus.

24. O Lord, arise and make me rich and blessed all round, in the name of Jesus.

25. Any evil power assigned to keep me out of my blessings, die, in the name of Jesus.

26. I withdraw my prosperity from controls of evil powers, in the name of Jesus.

27. Let heaven and earth reject every satanic verdict against me, in the name of Jesus.

28. I command the morning to reject every demonic work against me, in the name of Jesus.

29. Let the whole creature waste all my past, present and future problems, in the name of Jesus.

30. Any household witchcraft going on against me, be terminated, in the name of Jesus.

31. Any evil utterance made against my life, backfire, in the name of Jesus.

32. Owners of evil loads in my life carry your load, in the name of Jesus.

33. Devil, I command your works and that of your agents in my life to end, in the name of Jesus.

34. O God, release all manner of blessings into my life, in the name of Jesus.

35. Any prosperity of the devil in my life, catch fire and burn to ashes, in the name of Jesus.

FIRST STEP TO COMMAND THE MORNING

Prayer is a great privilege given to man by God. It is an address or petition to God in word or thought. It is an earnest request or wish. Prayer is an appeal from a child to the father. It is a man's soul desire for God, or a cry, supplication or an instinct that has utterance. It can be described as beseeching the Lord, or calling upon the Lord and lifting the heart. Prayer is pouring the heart and seeking the face of the Lord.

'*When thou saidst, seek ye my face; my heart said unto thee, thy face, Lord, will I seek*' (Psalms 27:8).

Prayer is a commandment from God to man.

'*Seek the Lord and his strength, seek his face continually*' (1 Chronicles 16:11).

We have in the bible what is called prayer as intercessions, which is praying for others.

'Cease not to give thanks for you, making mention of you in my prayers' (Ephesians 1:16).

God indeed commanded us to pray but prayers have steps, importance and levels. Misplacement of the priorities of prayers can result in loss of energy or waste of time. The first level of prayers which is the most important is the prayer of restoration of man back to God or prayer of repentance and forgiveness of sins. This is the foundational pillar of new and old testament prayers.

All other prayers without this foundational pillar in place, even prayers of command will amount to nothing. Cain prayed but he prayed outside the true foundation of prayer. His prayers had no substance. It is more of a complaint against curse placed upon him. There were no traces of regret, remorse, repentance, confession of sins or resolve to forsake his bad ways.

'And the Lord said unto Cain, where is Abel thy brother? And he said, I know not: Am I my brother's

*keeper? And he said, what hast thou done? the voice
of thy brother's blood crieth unto me from the ground.
And now art thou cursed from the earth, which hath
opened her mouth to receive thy brother's blood from
thy hand; When thou tillest the ground, it shall not
henceforth yield unto thee her strength; a fugitive and
a vagabond shalt thou be in the earth. And Cain said
unto the Lord, my punishment is greater than I can
bear. Behold, thou hast driven me out this day from
the face of the earth; and from thy face shall I be hid;
and I shall be a fugitive and a vagabond in the earth;
and it shall come to pass, that every one that findeth
me shall slay me. And the Lord said unto him,
therefore whosoever slayeth Cain, vengeance shall be
taken on him sevenfold. And the Lord set a mark
upon Cain, lest any finding him should kill him'*
(Genesis 4:9-15).

*'He that covereth his sins shall not prosper: but whoso
confesseth and forsaketh them shall have mercy'*
(Proverbs 28:13).

Cain complained to God against his punishment and untimely
death. Many people go to places of prayers to seek for
deliverance from suffering without plans to discontinue living in

sin. They have no thoughts of doing anything about their sinful lifestyles, yet they pray for long life and prosperity.

Praying for deliverance from problems and sufferings while regarding iniquity in your heart tantamount to deliberate neglect of foundational pillar that holds other prayers. Though it is prayer, it is outside God's true praying order. That was what Christ described as heathen prayers and hypocritical prayers against God's revealed will (*See* Matthew 6:7-8, 1 Kings 18:21-29, Luke 18:9-14, Psalms 106:13-15, 1 Samuel 8:6-9, Mark 17:25-26).

Some people believe in the number of prayers and commanding the morning without regard to quality or qualification. Others believe in prayer concerts without truly regarding God or His Word. People attend schools of prayer just to learn how to pray without authentically qualifying to pray. They do not regard God's Word or God Himself. They spend time learning about prayers and practice it to the disregard of many revealed will of God as prerequisites. Most people who pray and command the morning today pray with unforgiving spirits.

An unforgiving spirit is worse than cancer, Ebola, Coronavirus and HIV, yet they are neglected and ignored by many Christians, and even prayer warriors.

'Therefore, if thou bring thy gift to the altar, and there remembered that thy brother hath ought against thee; Leave there thy gift before the altar, and go thy way; first be reconciled to thy brother, and then come and offer thy gift. Agree with thine adversary quickly, whiles thou art in the way with him; lest at any time the adversary deliver thee to the judge, and the judge deliver thee to the officer, and thou be cast into prison. Verily I say unto thee, thou shalt by no means come out thence, till thou hast paid the uttermost farthing' (Matthew 5:23-26).

Many people are not faithful to thank God for all He has done for them already, yet they pray and complain to God asking for more. Such people are wicked and are an abomination unto God. You ought to be faithful with the little that God has given to you before praying for more.

'If I regard iniquity in my heart, the Lord will not hear me: But verily God hath heard me; he hath attended to the voice of my prayer. Blessed be God, which hath not turned away my prayer, nor his mercy from me' (Psalms 66:18-20).

If you are a sinner, God expects you to do away with every sin before any form of prayer. Many prayer and deliverance ministries gather sinners and teach them how to pray and command the morning without telling them they need to be born again. Such ministries, in a matter of time, produce more witches and wizards than all universities of witchcraft worldwide put together. The graduates of their prayer schools are more dangerous than danger itself.

Praying any kind of prayer in disrespect of what God's Word says is being rebellious and is practising of witchcraft. We have many prayer graduates today who are very zealous for prayers but disregard God's commandments. They are always in haste to start praying or go into prayer warfare against their enemies, but they will never obey God's Word. They are not bothered whether God is involved in their prayer meetings or not. They jump into prayer camps, bind, loose and command without God in the camps.

'*Then shall they call upon me, but I will not answer; they shall seek me early, but they shall not find me: For that they hated knowledge, and did not choose the fear of the Lord: They would none of my counsel: they despised all my reproof. Therefore, shall they eat of the fruit of their own way, and be filled with their own devices. For the turning away of the simple shall slay them, and the prosperity of fools shall destroy them'* (Proverbs 1:28-32).

Surprisingly, people can study very well and qualify as a graduate in the school of prayers without the Spirit of God with them. You can know the best language to use to call upon God or master how to seek God's face early, and yet fail to get answers to your prayers. When you despise God's way and knowledge, all your prayers of command will amount to nothing. When you fail to revere and fear God, your prayers will be waste.

Furthermore, when you reject God's counsel or despise his reproof, you will not make anything out of your prayers. Though you may obtain what you asked for and prosper in your prayer ministry, the end will be very painful. All your prosperity and exploits will become foolishness at the end.

'Whoso stoppeth his ears at the cry of the poor, he also shall cry himself, but shall not be heard' (Proverbs 21:13).

'Why should ye be stricken anymore? ye will revolt more and more: the whole head is sick, and the whole heart faint' (Isaiah 1:5).

'Ye ask, and receive not, because ye ask amiss, that ye may consume it upon your lusts' (James 4:3).

So many prayerful and influential people today are either very wicked in their hearts, or merciless and pitiless. They oppress the poor, kill others to take their possessions, and later turn around to pray to God. They shed innocent blood and deprive workers of their wages, and later go for prayers. If you must receive answers to your prayers, then you must have a true testimony of salvation. Your faith must be based on the Word of God. You must act and believe in God's Word, and maintain your confession. You must overcome fear, doubts, unbelief and discouragement for they are negative elements against God's holy Word and faith in Christ.

SECOND STEP TO COMMAND THE MORNING

Prayer of warfare or warfare prayer of command is another level of prayer. In warfare prayer of command, you can talk to or cry unto God, or beseech Him, but you cannot command or war against God. We command the creatures, war against principalities and powers in prayers of warfare.

'*For we wrestle not against flesh and blood, but against principalities, against powers, against the rulers of the darkness of this world, against spiritual wickedness in high places*' (Ephesians 6:12).

These are the spiritual powers that do not only stand against God and believers, but labour to convert the world into a battleground. That is why the Christian life is likened to 'wrestling' (*See* Ephesians 6:12); 'fighting' (*See* 1 Timothy 6:12, 1 Corinthians 9:25-27), 'warfare' (*See* 2 Corinthians 10:3-5).

Warfare is a time of wrestling with devil, principalities and against evil and wicked powers. It is also a time of fighting the good fight of faith to make sure you inherit eternal life. Before a believer gets to the highest level of prayer, he must be a good fighter of faith; someone who keeps and guides jealously his eternal life, maintaining his good profession of faith before many witnesses. Those who endeavour to attain the highest level of prayers must not be lukewarm believers. These are a group of Christians who have passed the first level and are qualified to receive answers from God. It is from this position they can begin like Paul to strive for masterly. By so doing, they command the morning, day and night. They are not ordinary Christians. They are people who are sure of their Salvation, sure of a place in heaven and a good relationship with God.

Such faithful and prayerful Christians can be equated to certificate and degree holders in prayer, who are striving for Masters in praying ministry and possibly, PhD. People like this are temperate in all things. They pursue holiness and seek for heart purify at all cost, even amid the fire of persecution, opposition, oppression, injustice, poverty, denial of fundamental human rights, slavery and bondage.

'And every man that striveth for the mastery is temperate in all things. Now they do it to obtain a

corruptible crown; but we an incorruptible. I therefore so run, not as uncertainly; so fight I, not as one that beateth the air: But I keep under my body, and bring it into subjection: lest that by any means, when I have preached to others, I myself should be a castaway' (1 Corinthians 9:25-27).

'And why stand we in jeopardy every hour? I protest by your rejoicing which I have in Christ Jesus our Lord, I die daily. If after the manner of men, I have fought with beasts at Ephesus, what advantageth it me, if the dead rise not? let us eat and drink; for tomorrow we die' (1 Corinthians 15:30-32).

In some cases, it is the other way around. They can be subjected to deception, slander, conspiracy, strife, criticism, betrayal, contention and division. At other times, it is trial and troubles that burn like fire to force them to surrender to the devil, but with Grace and God's restraining power they can stand for God to the end. These trials or tests come to reveal where our leaning is, and to grant us the opportunity to pray high-level prayers.

Trials and temptation can come through the subtle and clever creature, the devil. It can come through the closest person to you. It can come through familiarity, position and wealth. The wisdom of devil, the tempter, often makes temptation strong, difficult to recognize and hard to resist.

However, temptations do not necessarily come from people we do not know, love or respect only. Times have proven that some individuals who are honoured and respected more often transform to strong and irresistible temptations to their followers. Many leaders who have made themselves gods have been used by Satan to deceive their followers easily. Many have equally fallen into sin, condemnation and judgment and therefore cannot be favoured by God any longer, to pray high levels of prayers and be heard.

Your faith in Christ must be preserved and guarded regardless of any amount of temptation set before you. Keeping your faith alive in times of temptation qualifies you to partake in praying high levels of prayers. The Devil knows that your faith in God is a priceless treasure. He is ready to offer you the whole world in exchange for your faith, to rob you the opportunity of praying high-level prayers to obtain results.

Many people take the grace of God for granted. In times of trials, temptation, distress and perplexity faith must be fought for. Those who pray high levels of prayers to persevere. They do not allow threats of global recessions and impossibilities to sweep off their faith. They believe God in darkest hours when all foundations upon which men of this world built are being swept away ruthlessly.

Satan is behind all evil attempts to make believers fall from grace and fail God. He targets faithful Christians to hinder them from reaching high levels of effective prayers against his kingdom. He can use every means including people, things and circumstances available to pull you down. The Devil can do anything possible to stop you from praying to God. He can tempt you through the corrupted human heart, or entice you through your mind and eyes' gate. He can attack you through behaviours of evil companions or lead you into temptation and sin through the carelessness of your associates.

'*And Nahash the Ammonite answered them, on this condition will I make a covenant with you, that I may thrust out all your right eyes, and lay it for a reproach upon all Israel. And the elders of Jabesh said unto him, give us seven days' respite, that we may send messengers unto all the coasts of Israel: and then, if there be no man to save us, we will come out to thee. Then came the messengers to Gibeah of Saul, and told the tidings in the ears of the people: and all the people lifted up their voices, and wept. And, behold, Saul came after the herd out of the field; and Saul said, what aileth the people that they weep? And they told him the tidings of the men of Jabesh'* (1 Samuel 11:2-5).

Nevertheless, we are called to resist the devil and all his ways. Temptations come at any time in life to reveal inner strengths or weaknesses. Often, it is aimed for diversion and destruction, but you must resist the devil by any means.

' *Watch and pray, that ye enter not into temptation: the spirit indeed is willing, but the flesh is weak'* (Matthew 26:41).

'*My son, if sinners entice thee, consent thou not. If they say, Come with us, let us lay wait for blood, let us lurk privily for the innocent without cause: Let us swallow them up alive as the grave; and whole, as those that go down into the pit: We shall find all precious substance, we shall fill our houses with spoil: Cast in thy lot among us; let us all have one purse: My son, walk not thou in the way with them; refrain thy foot from their path'* (Proverbs 1:10-15).

Our Lord Jesus advised us to watch and pray so that we will not yield to temptations. He was victorious over every temptation because he was committed to pleasing God, the Father, in all things and at all times. You must resist, with all your strength, any endeavour by anyone to entice you into sin. You must reject whatever gifts sin presents to you, regardless of how great and precious the offers may appear. You must reject them all.

'*Then said his wife unto him, Dost thou still retain thine integrity? curse God, and die. But he said unto her, Thou speakest as one of the foolish women speaketh. What? shall we receive good at the hand of God, and shall we not receive evil? In all this did not Job sin with his lips*' (Job 2:9-10).

'*And I set before the sons of the house of the Rechabites pots full of wine, and cups, and I said unto them, Drink ye wine. But they said, we will drink no wine: for Jonadab the son of Rechab our father commanded us, saying, Ye shall drink no wine, neither ye, nor your sons forever*' (Jeremiah 35:5-6).

Temptations can come through people closest to you. Learn to refrain yourself and avoid their enticing offers. Victors recognize all enticing agents as God's enemies. Jesus resisted temptations with the written Word of God and overcame Satan. All manner of temptations must be resisted, whether they be of covetousness, lusts and fleshly gratification of the forbidden fruit.

However, if you have already fallen, you need to rise quickly and declare war against that particular sin, having confessed your sins and vowed to remain faithful to the end. You can join the army of God to pray high levels of prayers. You cannot continue in your sins and pray this kind of prayers. It is not possible.

'Behold, ye trust in lying words, that cannot profit' (Jeremiah 7:8).

Those who still steal, commit adultery, murder, swear falsely and commit all kinds of sins are not qualified to attain the highest level of prayer. God is looking for people who are purged; men of sound principles and saintly purposes to pray high levels of prayers and achieve great results.

THE HIGHEST LEVEL TO COMMAND THE MORNING

Many Christians do not know their rights and position in Christ. Others who know what God says about them in His Word do not believe God can be right. As a result, most Christians behave like slaves and beggars. Believers who are born again have a new life and are in partnership with Christ. Believers can become spiritually weak and unavailable when they do not take their rightful positions in Christ as sons of God.

'But as many as received him, to them gave he power to become the sons of God, even to them that believe on his name' (John 1:12).

'For as many as are led by the Spirit of God, they are the sons of God. For ye have not received the spirit of bondage again to fear; but ye have received the Spirit of adoption, whereby we cry, Abba, Father' (Romans 8:14-15).

'To redeem them that were under the law, that we might receive the adoption of sons' (Galatians 4:5).

God will never let down His children who are always conscious of who they are in Christ. When you value who God has made you in the grace of God, no one can undervalue you. When you take a stand of your place in Christ, the gates of hell can never prevail over you. It is an insult for a believer to accept lower class or position and remain poor, wretched and unworthy. When you know you worth, you will not accept any insult or allow the devil to push around in your life.

Believers are not only God's sons and daughters but are also members of Christ's body, new creation and beloved of God.

'*So, we, being many, are one body in Christ, and every one member one of another*' (*Romans 12:5*).

'*Therefore, if any man be in Christ, he is a new creature: old things are passed away; behold, all things are become new*' (2 Corinthians 5:17).

'*As the Father hath loved me, so have I loved you: continue ye in my love*' (John 15:9).

As a new creature, you are privileged to stand in God's presence as if you never committed any sin before. In positioning, we are younger brothers of Jesus and God's holy temples. Therefore, no demon or sickness has the power to defile God's holy temple. They are not allowed either to bring strange fire into God's temple.

'*And Nadab and Abihu, the sons of Aaron, took either of them his censer, and put fire therein, and put incense thereon, and offered strange fire before the Lord, which he commanded them not. And there went out fire from the Lord, and devoured them, and they died before the Lord*' (Leviticus 10:1-2).

No demon, witch or wizard has right to hurt you and go scot-free. As kings and queens, we must reign over all circumstances with our words and confessions that are powerful. Jesus empowered us to have authority over all the power of Satan and his agents on issues of our lives (*See* Luke 10:19). As kings and queens, we can unsay or undo whatever evil that was said or done against us.

'And from Jesus Christ, who is the faithful witness, and the first begotten of the dead, and the prince of the kings of the earth. Unto him that loved us, and washed us from our sins in his own blood, and hath made us kings and priests unto God and his Father; to him be glory and dominion for ever and ever. Amen' (Revelation 1:5-6).

'And if children, then heirs; heirs of God, and joint-heirs with Christ; if so be that we suffer with him, that we may be also glorified together.... He that spared not his own Son, but delivered him up for us all, how shall he not with him also freely give us all things?' (Romans 8:17, 32).

Our words as kings and queens, also heirs of God, are sovereign and superior to all other words on earth. Believers are sheep of the great shepherd, Jesus; eagles of the Lord and ambassadors of Christ on earth.

'I am the good shepherd: the good shepherd giveth his life for the sheep. But he that is an hireling, and not the shepherd, whose own the sheep are not, seeth the wolf coming, and leaveth the sheep, and fleeth: and

the wolf catcheth them, and scattereth the sheep. The hireling fleeth, because he is an hireling, and careth not for the sheep. I am the good shepherd, and know my sheep, and am known of mine. As the Father knoweth me, even so know I the Father: and I lay down my life for the sheep' (John 10:11-15).

Accepting failure means accepting that God is a failure too. This will never be the case. Jesus did not mince words in confessing who He is even at the cross. It did not matter who believed or doubted Him. He simply took His stand in God. It is unacceptable for believers, as God's ambassadors, to belittle God. For an American president to come to a country in Africa and be insulted or intimidated, especially when he did nothing wrong, is an insult to the American government. He represents America wherever he goes. American ambassadors all over the world cannot accept insults either or belittle their nation in the face of an empty threat from one local leader.

'Now then we are ambassadors for Christ, as though God did beseech you by us: we pray you in Christ's stead, be ye reconciled to God' (2 Corinthians 5:20).

Believers are not American government ambassadors but are ambassadors of Christ, God. Believers are empowered to follow Christ's steps. As an ambassador of Christ, you are expected to talk or walk like Him and to take a stand to maintain the kingdom's principles and values anywhere in the world you go.

COMMAND FROM THE HEAVENLIES

True Christian believers are exalted and positioned in Christ. They have risen with Christ, and have been quickened and made alive in Christ.

> '*If ye then be risen with Christ, seek those things which are above, where Christ sitteth on the right hand of God*' (Colossians 3:1).

When Jesus Christ was raised from the dead by the power of God, the stone covering the tomb was rolled away. Believers rose together with Him to ascend into heaven. At that point, all dominion of satanic kingdoms and domain were dismantled. Organized enmity in Satan's domain was removed. Believers at that moment recovered the image of God lost by Adam in the Garden of Eden.

> '*And God said, Let us make man in our image, after our likeness: and let them have dominion over the fish of the sea, and over the fowl of the air, and over the*

cattle, and over all the earth, and over every creeping thing that creepeth upon the earth. So, God created man in his own image, in the image of God created he him; male and female created he them. And God blessed them, and God said unto them, Be fruitful, and multiply, and replenish the earth, and subdue it: and have dominion over the fish of the sea, and over the fowl of the air, and over every living thing that moveth upon the earth' (Genesis 1:26-28).

Jesus Christ still reigns with true believers spiritually. An unbeliever or sinner cannot comprehend this miracle. When a sinner repents and prays to God through Christ, believing that Jesus Christ has borne all guilt and suppressed penalties of sins, transformation takes place immediately. Such a person becomes spiritually alive and sits together in heavenly places with Christ, whose operations on earth become more heavenly than earthly. As long as you are in covenant with God, you are above all creatures and can use them to fight in prayer.

'*And hath raised us up together, and made us sit together in heavenly places in Christ Jesus'* (Ephesians 2:6).

Secondly, the devil and his agents together with all sinners remain on the lower side. Those who enter into covenant with Satan sit with him in the second heaven, which is also the atmospheric heaven. While they operate from the second heaven, believers operate and control all things from the third heaven.

> '*Blotting out the handwriting of ordinances that was against us, which was contrary to us, and took it out of the way, nailing it to his cross; And having spoiled principalities and powers, he made a shew of them openly, triumphing over them in it* (Colossians 2:14-15).

The death and resurrection of Christ dealt with all your trespasses, overturned control of all evil powers and positioned God's children above the devil and all his agents. Christ is the head of principalities and powers. He is in charge of everything including powers in heaven, under the heavens and on the earth. He controls thrones, dominions, principalities, powers and all things.

'For by him were all things created, that are in heaven, and that are in earth, visible and invisible, whether they be thrones, or dominions, or principalities, or powers: all things were created by him, and for him: And he is before all things, and by him all things consist. And he is the head of the body, the church: who is the beginning, the firstborn from the dead; that in all things he might have the preeminence. For it pleased the Father that in him should all fulness dwell; And, having made peace through the blood of his cross, by him to reconcile all things unto himself; by him, I say, whether they be things in earth, or things in heaven' (Colossians 1:16-20).

As devil and his agents, all heaven elements, earth and all things have been put under Christ, so have they all been put under believers' feet, who are risen with Christ and seated together with Him in heavenly places. It is, therefore, wrong for any believer to bow down before or take orders from the devil and his agents, instead of giving them command.

THE COSTLY IGNORANCE

Idolatry is bowing down before and worshipping carved or painted images, or sacrificing to such images, or worshipping other gods and swearing by such gods. It also means walking after other gods, speaking in their names, looking up to those gods while serving and fearing such gods. Worshipping the true God with an image is idolatry. Worshipping of angels, the host of heavens, devil and his agents, dead people, as well as setting up idols in the heart, covetousness and sensuality are all forms of idolatry.

Idolatry is a costly ignorance. Man was and still is, the crown of God's creation made only a little lower than the angels.

'*For thou hast made him a little lower than the angels, and hast crowned him with glory and honor*' (Psalms 8:5).

From the beginning of Christ's public ministry until the time He went to the cross, He did not bow to any other creature. It is a costly ignorance for believers who are seated in heavenly places with Christ to bow down and worship the devil or any other creature.

THE DEVIL'S WISDOM

Lucifer having been in the third heaven is informed of such power as was invested into man. He knows that man has power over all other creatures. Therefore, the devil teaches all evil covenant agents on how to use creatures to fight and subvert man's authority. He teaches his agents how to use elements in the heavenlies to fight God's people. These elements are meant to be used by believers but as a result of ignorance many believers do not know how to use them.

Devil now teaches his agents and occultic people how to use these elements against God's children. Elements of the heavenlies include - sun, moon, stars, water and the elements. We have four major elements.

- Water
- Fire
- Air
- Earth

These elements have no enemies, especially fire. An enemy can use your fire to destroy you and it will not refuse. Once a fire is put in motion, it will not recognize its owner or practice discrimination. The air, on the other hand, can go anywhere. It is neither solid nor substantial. It can carry any message anywhere, even against ignorant children of God.

When an occultic person employs air, water, fire or uses the earth against you and you do not know how to counter the air, water, fire and earth, or redirect their services, you will be harmed.

These elements are created for your use but due to ignorance, the devil and his agents are instead using them against you, and these elements do obey for they cannot discriminate. If you cannot use what God has provided for you, another person may use it against you. When an occultic man bows down to an image and speaks to it, it can hear and act for the occultic man. The reason is that all creations have ears. There is always a spirit behind any spiritual or physical organization. That is why people who have learnt how to command the morning and address the elements rule this world in place of believers.

Any wicked person who knows how to use the heavenlies can be very wicked and dangerous. There is a difference between praying and fighting from heaven. When a believer is praying from heaven, he is talking to God, reminding Him of His promises and making requests. But when a believer is fighting from heaven, he is taking authority over the works of the devil and his agents and all activities of dark powers under heaven.

'Then spake Joshua to the Lord in the day when the Lord delivered up the Amorites before the children of Israel, and he said in the sight of Israel, Sun, stand thou still upon Gibeon; and thou, Moon, in the valley of Ajalon' (Joshua 10:12).

In the above verse, Joshua prayed from heaven's position first before fighting. He spoke to God, reminding Him of His promise of giving them victory over the Amorites before the day runs out. Thereafter, he took authority over natural elements and they obeyed. So, the highest level of prayer is fighting from the heavens' positions. Praying from the heavens is talking to God while fighting from heaven's position to address evil forces and command the whole creatures to obey their Creator.

4

Commanding from the Heavenlies

I like to divide this section into two sub-topics; Prayer of Authority and Prayer of Decree. These two are like identical twins but slightly different.

Prayer of Authority: This is making a conclusive statement or set of statements and taking official decisions when someone is in authority. A person in authority can use power to influence others and command direction of thought, opinion and behaviours. Prayer of authority is a right given to every believer.

Prayer of Decree: True Believers can authoritatively decree a thing through prayer and it comes to pass. In a decree, a believer can give orders and the orders will be enforced. True believers have authority to pray and decree a thing and they will stand.

Both of these prayers of fighting from the heavenlies are identical and are high-level prayers, which have been granted to believers by God through His son, our Lord Jesus Christ.

'And I will give unto thee the keys of the kingdom of heaven: and whatsoever thou shalt bind on earth shall be bound in heaven: and whatsoever thou shalt loose on earth shall be loosed in heaven... Verily I say unto you, Whatsoever ye shall bind on earth shall be bound in heaven: and whatsoever ye shall loose on earth shall be loosed in heaven' (Matthew 16:19, 18:18).

'Behold, I give unto you power to tread on serpents and scorpions, and over all the power of the enemy: and nothing shall by any means hurt you' (Luke 10:19).

Jesus gave us authority to bind anything on earth and they are bound in heaven, and to lose anything on earth and they are loosed in heaven. This can be done through prayers of authority and decree. Jesus' disciples tried it when Jesus was with them and it worked. They tried it after His resurrection and it worked. Today, the same authority to command still works for as many that believe.

'And heal the sick that are therein, and say unto them, the kingdom of God is come nigh unto you... And he said unto him, Arise, go thy way: thy faith hath made thee whole' (Luke 10:9, 17-19).

Power to take authority over Satan our enemy and all his works has been invested into all believers. When you pray authoritatively, the devil and his agents are subjected to obey you. You can use the name of Jesus Christ to tread upon serpents, scorpions and all the power of the enemy. Every creature is made subject to believers and is bound to obey believers' voices of command at all times. The name of Christ is so powerful that no other power can stand against it.

'And these signs shall follow them that believe; In my name shall they cast out devils; they shall speak with new tongues; They shall take up serpents; and if they drink any deadly thing, it shall not hurt them; they shall lay hands on the sick, and they shall recover' (Mark 16:17-18).

You can use the name of Jesus Christ to cast out demons, heal the sick and do many marvellous works against Satan's kingdom. In a prayer of decree, if you would issue any decree using the name of Jesus, it will be done as long as it will glorify God, the Father. God promises to do anything we ask in the name of Jesus.

'And whatsoever ye shall ask in my name, that will I do, that the Father may be glorified in the Son. If ye shall ask any thing in my name, I will do it... Ye have not chosen me, but I have chosen you, and ordained you, that ye should go and bring forth fruit, and that your fruit should remain: that whatsoever ye shall ask of the Father in my name, he may give it you.... And in that day ye shall ask me nothing. Verily, verily, I say unto you, Whatsoever ye shall ask the Father in my name, he will give it you. Hitherto have ye asked nothing in my name: ask, and ye shall receive, that your joy may be full (John 14:13-14, 15:16, 16:23-24).

You have the right to use the name of Jesus in prayers of authority and decree. You only need to know some few things that will help you to effectively use your authority. Lack of certain knowledge has weakened many people's prayers of authority or command.

5

God, The Creator of the Universe

From the beginning, God created the heaven and the earth, without any assistance or contributions from any creature that was created.

'*In the beginning God created the Heaven and the earth.... And he blessed him, and said, blessed be Abram of the most high God, possessor of heaven and earth: And blessed be the most high God, which hath delivered thine enemies into thy hand. And he gave him tithes of all. And the king of Sodom said unto Abram, give me the persons, and take the goods to thyself. And Abram said to the king of Sodom, I have lift up mine hand unto the Lord, the most high God, the possessor of heaven and earth'* (Genesis 1:1, 14:19-22).

God did not create the heaven and earth to be run by the devil and his agents. He owns and possesses heaven and earth, and created man to take care of the earth. Moses proved to Pharaoh that the earth does not belong to him but the LORD's.

'*And Moses said unto him, as soon as I am gone out of the city, I will spread abroad my hands unto the Lord; and the thunder shall cease, neither shall there be any more hail; that thou mayest know how that the earth is the Lord's.... Now therefore, if ye will obey my voice indeed, and keep my covenant, then ye shall be a peculiar treasure unto me above all people: for all the earth is mine'* (Exodus 9:29, 19:5)

The heavens, the earth and the sea, and entire creatures in them are all created and owned by the Lord.

'For in six days the Lord made heaven and earth, the sea, and all that in them is, and rested the seventh day: wherefore the Lord blessed the Sabbath day, and hallowed it' (Exodus 20:11).

'Behold, the heaven and the heaven of heavens is the Lord's thy God, the earth also, with all that therein is' (Deuteronomy 10:14).

'But who am I, and what is my people, that we should be able to offer so willingly after this sort? for all things come of thee, and of thine own have we given thee. For we are strangers before thee, and sojourners, as were all our fathers: our days on the earth are as a shadow, and there is none abiding. O Lord our God, all this store that we have prepared to build thee an house for thine holy name cometh of thine hand, and is all thine own' (1 Chronicles 29:14-16).

Without God, no man can amount to anything. Therefore, those that do not honour God with their lives and substances amount to nothing. All that a man has and will ever have to belong to God. You do not have the right to use anything on earth without God's permission and to God's glory. You brought nothing into this world and will not take anything away as you leave. God owns all the earth and the fullness thereof. He owns life, fame and possession.

All the earth and the heavens and all their fullness belong to God of creation. You will not yield enough for God with your life except you let God have the absolute ownership of your life without rival. Those who have refused to give themselves to God through Christ Jesus are robbing God of what rightly belongs to Him. You have to worship God through investing your time, money and talents on God, as His Word and will demand. Otherwise, you cannot glorify His name and you lose your right of dominion over creatures and to enjoy their services on earth.

Devil, the master usurper, has subtly deceived people into believing his lies concerning who owns the earth. He is using creatures to fight God and the saints. He has kept believers in ignorance for many years. All who have refused to give themselves to God through Christ Jesus are robbing God. Believers, as a result of ignorance, have allowed wicked people to occupy thrones on earth and manage the wealth of the earth, and suppress Truth.

'*For by him were all things created, that are in heaven, and that are in earth, visible and invisible, whether they be thrones, or dominions, or principalities, or powers: all things were created by him, and for him: And he is before all things, and by him all things consist. And he is the head of the body, the church: who is the beginning, the firstborn from the dead; that in all things he might have the preeminence. For it pleased the Father that in him should all fulness dwell* (Colossians 1:16-19).

All things were created through Jesus Christ; things in heaven and on the earth, visible and invisible, thrones, dominions, principalities and powers. They were all created by Jesus and are for Jesus. Therefore, the church and all believers are to rule and control things in heaven and the earth, instead of devil, occultic and satanic agents.

'For none of us liveth to himself, and no man dieth to himself. For whether we live, we live unto the Lord; and whether we die, we die unto the Lord: whether we live therefore, or die, we are the Lord's. For to this end Christ both died, and rose, and revived, that he might be Lord both of the dead and living. But why dost thou judge thy brother? or why dost thou set at nought thy brother? for we shall all stand before the judgment seat of Christ. For it is written, As I live, saith the Lord, every knee shall bow to me, and every tongue shall

confess to God. So, then every one of us shall give account of himself to God (Romans 14:7-12).

'*And he said also unto his disciples, there was a certain rich man, which had a steward; and the same was accused unto him that he had wasted his goods. And he called him, and said unto him, how is it that I hear this of thee? give an account of thy stewardship; for thou mayest be no longer steward.... He that is faithful in that which is least is faithful also in much: and he that is unjust in the least is unjust also in much. If therefore ye have not been faithful in the unrighteous mammon, who will commit to your trust the true riches? And if ye have not been faithful in that which is another man's, who shall give you that which is your own? No servant can serve two masters: for either he will hate the one, and love the other; or else he will hold to the one, and despise the other. Ye cannot serve God and mammon*' (Luke 16:1-2, 10-13).

Believers who fail to manager their Father's possessions on earth will not blame God. It is the believers' duties to manage and control all created things. It is not the duty of the wicked. Positions of leadership are meant for believers. Believers will surely account to God how they used and managed the earth, the heavens and all creatures to advance God's kingdom. If believers allow Satan and his agents to use the sun, moon, stars, waters and other elements against God, they cannot blame God.

You have the right to use fire, air, water and earth to defend yourself and fight the devil to frustrate all his works on earth. When you as believers ignore to use these things, wicked people can use them to destroy you and you cannot blame God. The creatures themselves cannot be happy that believers are not making use of them to fight the wicked.

Some of these elements, like fire, do not discriminate. They have no enemies and they eagerly want to be used for action. So, when you as a believer do not know how to use them, the wicked can use them against you and they will obey the wicked. They can only say '*no*' to the wicked when they hear commands of superior officers (*believers*).

'*For the earnest expectation of the creature waiteth for the manifestation of the sons of God*' (Romans 8:19).

'*Hast thou commanded the morning since thy days; and caused the dayspring to know his place; That it might take hold of the ends of the earth, that the wicked might be shaken out of it?*' (Job 38:12-13).

The earnest expectation of the whole creature waits for you to put them to use. Creatures value believers' words of authority more than words of the wicked. The cloud, tempest, thunder, lightning, hailstone, rain, snow dew and even all that belongs to your enemies are waiting for you to use them. You can command all things on earth and heaven to rise and fight for you. You can reverse all statements of the wicked against them. The creatures are earnestly waiting for your command as a believer.

The prodigal son's brother did not know his right, and as a result, his younger brother used what belonged to him to enjoy and throw parties. Many believers on earth remain to suffer while allowing the wicked people to utilize the morning, day and other creatures to control and waste their destinies.

6

The Portion of the Wicked – I

G od made provisions for everyone on earth to access best of things of life including the wicked. He sent His Son Jesus Christ not to condemn the world but to convince, convict and convert all men.

'*For God sent not his Son into the world to condemn the world; but that the world through him might be saved.... She said, No man, Lord. And Jesus said unto her, neither do I condemn thee: go, and sin no more*' (John 3:17, 8:11).

God's ultimate purpose for sending His beloved Son is to save the world through Him. No man has the right to judge or condemn whom God has not condemned. Jesus desires to see every sinner saved and go to sin no more.

> ' *Ye are of your father the devil, and the lusts of your father ye will do. He was a murderer from the beginning, and abode not in the truth, because there is no truth in him. When he speaketh a lie, he speaketh of his own: for he is a liar, and the father of it.... Then Jesus said unto them, my time is not yet come: but your time is always ready. The world cannot hate you; but me it hateth, because I testify of it, that the works thereof are evil.... And when he is come, he will reprove the world of sin, and of righteousness, and of judgment* (John 7:6-7, 8:44, 16:8)

By the power of the Holy Spirit, any sinner who yields to Christ through the gospel will be convinced that Jesus is Lord. The Holy Spirit convicts' sinners of sin and enables them to avoid it. When sinners hear the Word of God and get convinced, convicted and converted, they will escape eternal condemnation and God's judgment. Sinners are not automatically condemned as wicked people until they refuse to believe the gospel of Jesus Christ.

> '*He that believeth on him is not condemned: but he that believeth not is condemned already, because he hath not believed in the name of the only begotten Son of God.... He that believeth on the Son hath everlasting life: and he that believeth not the Son shall not see life; but the wrath of God abideth on him*' (John 3:18, 36).

Unbelief in the gospel of Jesus Christ brings condemnation. It is a great sin to reject the gospel of Jesus Christ for it is the ultimate reason for eternal condemnation. When one hears the gospel and rejects it, a mark of condemnation is placed upon that person. The wrath of God abides with such people and they will lose eternal life. People who hate Christ and the gospel walk in darkness.

> '*Who knowing the judgment of God, that they which commit such things are worthy of death, not only do*

the same, but have pleasure in them that do them' (Romans 1:32).

These are people who are condemned already for they believed not, but rather loved darkness, do evil, hate the light and refused to come to light.

'For every one that doeth evil hateth the light, neither cometh to the light, lest his deeds should be reproved' (John 3:20).

If you are afraid of being reproved of sin or you despise being saved, you are not only condemned but also classified as wicked.

'Verily, verily, I say unto you, He that believeth on me hath everlasting life' (John 6:47).

'Therefore, being justified by faith, we have peace with God through our Lord Jesus Christ' (Romans 5:1).

The only way to escape eternal judgment and damnation is to believe in and confess Christ, and subsequently come to light having the assurance that Jesus has forsaken your sins and have removed your guilt and condemnation. You have to believe that Jesus can save, cleanse, make and keep holy, and answer all prayers.

'Therefore, I say unto you, what things soever ye desire, when ye pray, believe that ye receive them, and ye shall have them' (Mark 11:24).

But when a sinner rejects the offer of salvation, he or she is grouped among the wicked. Until he or she repents and accepts Christ, they remain wicked.

7

The Portion of the Wicked – II

Regardless of whatever pleasures a sinner and wicked person enjoy in the present, a day is set aside for his or her life to be put out, and the spark of his or her fire shall not shine. Believers who know the portion of the wicked will not allow the wicked to reign over them, or torment them for too long. But when you know your right as a believer, you can put out the light of the wicked and the spark of their fire. You can darken their altars and put out their candles. You can destroy the wicked together with their counsel and cast them down.

'Yea, the light of the wicked shall be put out, and the spark of his fire shall not shine. The light shall be dark in his tabernacle, and his candle shall be put out with him. The steps of his strength shall be straitened, and his own counsel shall cast him down. For he is cast into a net by his own feet, and he walketh upon a snare... His remembrance shall perish from the earth, and he shall have no name in the street' (Job 18:5-8, 17).

Believers who can pray high levels of prayers can command the wicked to walk into nets, snares and traps the wicked have set. You can command terror against them from every side. You can root out their confidence. Believers can deal with the wicked and wipe out their remembrance. A cleverly wicked person can be exposed using high levels of prayers. You can command the heavens to expose and reveal hidden iniquities of the wicked on the earth.

'The heaven shall reveal his iniquity; and the earth shall rise up against him' (Job 20:27).

'For in the hand of the Lord there is a cup, and the wine is red; it is full of mixture; and he poureth out of

the same: but the dregs thereof, all the wicked of the earth shall wring them out, and drink them' (Psalms 75:8).

You can command the mouth of the wicked to open and drink the cup of judgment. True believers can ask the earth to consume the wicked by opening its mouth to swallow them up. The wicked are meant to be out off from the earth (*See* Psalms 75:8, 104:35).

The righteous are not permitted to vacate the earth for the wicked. The earth is destined to swallow the wicked. Believers should, therefore, master how to deal with the wicked, and command them to inherit their destinies and go to where they have been assigned to. It was a big mistake for Abel to allow Cain to live while he died prematurely. The question, therefore, is - how do we deal with the wicked-on earth?

8

Dealing with the Wicked

A wicked person who despises the mercy of God becomes obstinate and ends up with a reprobate mind deserves the divine judgment of God.

'*For the wrath of God is revealed from heaven against all ungodliness and unrighteousness of men, who hold the truth in unrighteousness; Because that which may be known of God is manifest in them; for God hath shewed it unto them. For the invisible things of him from the creation of the world are clearly seen, being understood by the things that are made, even his eternal power and Godhead; so that they are without excuse: Because that, when they knew God, they glorified him not as God, neither were thankful; but became vain in their imaginations, and their foolish heart was darkened. Professing themselves to be wise, they became fools, and changed the glory of the uncorruptible God into an image made like to corruptible man, and to birds, and four-footed beasts, and creeping things. Wherefore God also gave them up to uncleanness through the lusts of their own hearts, to dishonor their own bodies between themselves.... And even as they did not like to retain God in their knowledge, God gave them over to a reprobate mind, to do those things which are not convenient*' (Romans 1:18-24, 28).

When a person sells his or her soul to devil and vows, in covenant with the devil, to perpetrate evil in a lifetime, such a wicked person can be very dangerous. Given any opportunity, such people can be very destructive. They can waste a whole nation and it will satisfy them. Such people have no natural affection because they have the fullness of the devil inside them. Their original selves are incarnated by the devil to pursue a satanic agenda.

'*For this cause God gave them up unto vile affections: for even their women did change the natural use into that which is against nature: And likewise also the men, leaving the natural use of the woman, burned in their lust one toward another; men with men working that which is unseemly, and receiving in themselves that recompence of their error which was meet* (Romans 1:26-27).

'*And there was given unto him a mouth speaking great things and blasphemies; and power was given unto him to continue forty and two months. And he opened his mouth in blasphemy against God, to blaspheme his name, and his tabernacle, and them that dwell in heaven*' (Revelation 13:5-6).

You can deal with this level of wicked people with high-level prayers. To pray to the highest level of prayer, you need to employ and involve all creatures to appear on the battlefield. You may need to use the most destructive words or language on earth to war against every wicked people. A wicked person who has not attained a reprobate state is likely to repent and turn back to God. If you could start praying high-level prayers, most wicked people attacking you will quickly abandon the camp of devil.

'But Elymas the sorcerer (for so is his name by interpretation) withstood them, seeking to turn away the deputy from the faith. Then Saul, (who also is called Paul,) filled with the Holy Ghost, set his eyes on him, And said, O full of all subtilty and all mischief, thou child of the devil, thou enemy of all righteousness, wilt thou not cease to pervert the right ways of the Lord? And now, behold, the hand of the Lord is upon thee, and thou shalt be blind, not seeing the sun for a season. And immediately there fell on him a mist and a darkness; and he went about seeking some to lead him by the hand. Then the deputy, when he saw what was done, believed, being astonished at the doctrine of the Lord' (Acts 13:8-12).

When people like Elymas are allowed to see each day and walk freely on earth, they can convert a whole nation for the devil and block millions of people from entering heaven. However, this statement is not an endorsement for believers to judge the wicked unto death without first giving them the opportunity to be born again. Simon the sorcerer was a deceived and evil wizard with the ability to bewitch a whole city.

'But there was a certain man, called Simon, which before time in the same city used sorcery, and bewitched the people of Samaria, giving out that himself was some great one: To whom they all gave heed, from the least to the greatest, saying, This man is the great power of God. And to him they had regard, because that of long time he had bewitched them with sorceries. But when they believed Philip preaching the things concerning the kingdom of God, and the name of Jesus Christ, they were baptized, both men and women' (<u>Acts 8:9-12</u>).

He used his sorcery to bewitch the people of Samaria. He was highly respected. No one in that city, big or small, questioned his source of power. Rather he was regarded as one who got power from God. He ruled and reigned in the city of Samaria for a very long time without any rival or confrontation from any other power (*See* <u>Acts 8:12-17</u>).

When Philip, the evangelist, came with power from the most high God, he preached concerning the kingdom of God as none had preached before. Some people can still learn how to pray well even when they do not belong to God's kingdom. They learn how to pray high-level prayers without being born again. They learn also how to use dangerous weapons to kill witches and wizards using the name of Jesus Christ and possibly cast out demons when they are yet to become God's children. Such prayer warriors and deliverance ministers are taking high and dangerous risks.

'Then certain of the vagabond Jews, exorcists, took upon them to call over them which had evil spirits the name of the Lord Jesus, saying, we adjure you by Jesus whom Paul preacheth. And there were seven sons of one Sceva, a Jew, and chief of the priests, which did so. And the evil spirit answered and said, Jesus I know, and Paul I know; but who are ye? And the man in whom the evil spirit was leaped on them, and overcame them, and prevailed against them, so that they fled out of that house naked and wounded' (Acts 19:13-16).

You must first secure your place in heaven to pray high-level prayers. It is only those who have their names written in the book of life that can pray for the wicked and they repent and turn away from evil. However, in dealing with the wicked through high-level prayers, we must always let God decide the final fate of the wicked.

' Then Simon himself believed also: and when he was baptized, he continued with Philip, and wondered, beholding the miracles and signs which were done.... And when Simon saw that through laying on of the apostles' hands the Holy Ghost was given, he offered them money, Saying, give me also this power, that on whomsoever I lay hands, he may receive the Holy Ghost. But Peter said unto him, thy money perish with thee, because thou hast thought that the gift of God may be purchased with money. Thou hast neither part nor lot in this matter: for thy heart is not right in the sight of God. Repent therefore of this thy wickedness, and pray God, if perhaps the thought of thine heart may be forgiven thee. For I perceive that thou art in the gall of bitterness, and in the bond of iniquity. Then answered Simon, and said, pray ye to the Lord for me, that none of these things which ye have spoken come upon me' (Acts 8:13, 18-24).

A wicked person can only escape the judgment of God if he or she repents, regardless of how long he or she has worked for the devil. Philip gave Simon an option to repent of his wickedness and pray to God to be forgiven. A curse was placed upon him because he was in the gall of bitterness and the bond of iniquity. Most believers go to the extreme in praying against wicked people without giving them the option of repentance and forgiveness of their sins. Others pray for the wicked to live long and cause more harm on earth. They too are in the extreme.

The world would have been better if Cain had died instead of Abel. It is better to pray that the wicked be not allowed to see the next day with their eyes or live longer perpetrating more evil. However, the option to spare the wicked or eliminate them belongs to God alone. The truth is that if you know how to pray high-level prayers, the righteous will not die while the wicked lives long.

A righteous person who does not know how to pray high-level prayers, but always pray that God will bless the wicked, spare and give them long life may not live long on the earth. If Moses had not prayed and challenged the wicked people of his time, he would have died prematurely while his enemies lived long to do more wicked. But he reported matters to God and God responded.

'And Moses was very wroth, and said unto the Lord,
Respect not thou their offering: I have not taken one
ass from them, neither have I hurt one of them.... And
there came out a fire from the Lord, and consumed

the two hundred and fifty men that offered incense' (Numbers 16:15, 35).

In Paul's time, certain Jews banded together and bound themselves under a curse saying that they would neither eat nor drink till they kill Paul. They were more than forty people who entered into a conspiracy.

> '*And when it was day, certain of the Jews banded together, and bound themselves under a curse, saying that they would neither eat nor drink till they had killed Paul. And they were more than forty which had made this conspiracy. And they came to the chief priests and elders, and said, we have bound ourselves under a great curse, that we will eat nothing until we have slain Paul. Now therefore ye with the council signify to the chief captain that he bring him down unto you tomorrow, as though ye would inquire something more perfectly concerning him: and we, or ever he come near, are ready to kill him*' (Acts 23:12-15).

Many people enter into a covenant with the devil to kill others. They use numerous evil means to waste peoples' lives to make many gains. They excel in making other people useless by trading with their destinies.

'*And it came to pass, as we went to prayer, a certain damsel possessed with a spirit of divination met us, which brought her masters much gain by soothsaying: The same followed Paul and us, and cried, saying, These men are the servants of the most high God, which shew unto us the way of salvation. And this did she many days. But Paul, being grieved, turned and said to the spirit, I command thee in the name of Jesus Christ to come out of her. And he came out the same hour. And when her masters saw that the hope of their gains was gone, they caught Paul and Silas, and drew them into the marketplace unto the rulers*' (Acts 16:16-19).

If Paul had not cast out the demon that multiplied the business of that occultic grandmaster, he would have continued to make many gains with the young girl's destiny. Again, if Paul had not done something concerning the people that entered into a bond to kill him, he would have died before fulfilling his ministry.

'*And when Paul's sister's son heard of their lying-in wait, he went and entered into the castle, and told Paul. Then Paul called one of the centurions unto him, and said, bring this young man unto the chief captain: for he hath a certain thing to tell him. So, he took him, and brought him to the chief captain, and said, Paul the prisoner called me unto him, and prayed me to bring this young man unto thee, who hath something to say unto thee. Then the chief captain took him by the hand, and went with him aside privately, and asked him, what is that thou hast to tell me? And he said, The Jews have agreed to desire thee that thou wouldest bring down Paul tomorrow into the council, as though they would inquire somewhat of him more perfectly. But do not thou yield unto them: for there lie in wait for him of them more than forty men, which have bound themselves with an oath, that they will neither eat nor drink till they have killed him: and now are they ready, looking for a promise from thee*' (Acts 23:16-21).

High-level prayers can frustrate the wicked and keep true believers alive to fulfil their ministries on earth.

9

How to Command every Creature

A believer must position him or herself in heaven to pray to the highest level of prayers. Your understanding must be enlightened to know Christ who has called you. You must enter fully into the riches of Christ's glory to inherit what rightly belongs to you as a saint. You must also be conscious that you have Christ's supreme power working in you. You must believe that you are operating from the heavenly places far above every other dominion or principality. This high position will enable you to crush every opposition from any part of creation (*See* Ephesians 1:18-23).

'And hath raised us up together, and made us sit together in heavenly places in Christ Jesus' (Ephesians 2:6).

Fighting from heavenly places puts you far above all dark powers. It is not a battle you fight while under the control or influence of any evil kingdom. They will bring you down and disgrace you if you should try it. Would they choose not to disgrace you immediately, they will empower you with evil to use you and later dehumanize you for eternity. The heavenlies are the centre of all spiritual warfare against the devil. God and his saints rule the universe from the heavens.

'The Lord hath prepared his throne in the heavens; and his kingdom ruleth over all' (Psalms 103:19).

Heavens is the place of believers' position in Christ and all angelic activities. It is also the battlefield for all spiritual warfare. Any battle won in the heavenlies is won forever. When you, as a believer, speak from the heavenlies, you are in control. Speaking from the heavenlies means exercising dominion and reigning over all your enemies. Curses issued from heaven are very dangerous.

When you fight from heavens' position, the sun, moon, stars, waters and all elements will carry your words to fulfilment. Wicked and occultic people draw powers from the sun, moon, etc. But when believers issue commands, every evil command prostrates. It can be likened to commands of a local leader crashing with presidential orders.

In the absence of believers' commands, the heavens carry orders from whoever knows how to use them. The elements, like fire, do not discriminate. They have no enemies. Fire is very effective and penetrative while in action. It has high purging effect and burning quality. However, the fire sent by any wicked person comes with less power. The effective quality of fire from satanic kingdom weakens when confronted by a believer who fights with fire.

A believer who knows how to fight with air cannot be trapped for God's angels can pass him or her through any substance when fighting from the heavenlies. Such a believer can be more powerful than Satan for his or her movements will uncertain and unpredictable. Wicked people are always afraid of believers who fight from the heavens using the air. Air has no solid or substance and thus can enter any dark kingdom or witchcraft conference hall without announcement to wreak havoc on the wicked.

Believers have the power to enter the cloud, tempest, thunder, lightning, hail storm rain, snow and dew. However, any speech or utterance could be dangerous and destructive while moving with these creatures. Gates, doors, keys, spiritual and physical soldiers cannot stop you when you are moving with the above creatures. When you are dealing with a problem that comes from the waters, you can use the tempest mixed with water against them, and they will bow. You can command the dept to rise against the powers from the waters that are against your life.

No life on earth can survive without water. It is abundant on earth and can be very destructive. You can command the waters to fight your battle and trouble your troubles unto death. When you fight from the heavens, all creatures will obey you without negotiation.

.

'*And whereas they commanded to leave the stump of the tree roots; thy kingdom shall be sure unto thee, after that thou shalt have known that the heavens do rule*' (Daniel 4:26).

'*Immediately after the tribulation of those days shall the sun be darkened, and the moon shall not give her light, and the stars shall fall from heaven, and the powers of the heavens shall be shaken'* (Matthew 24:29).

You can withdraw the services of the sun, moon, stars and any creature from the wicked. You can ask the morning, the day, month or year to deny the wicked in the land peace. Believers who know their rights can stop the earth from serving the wicked.

'Hear, O heavens, and give ear, O earth: for the Lord hath spoken, I have nourished and brought up children, and they have rebelled against me' (Isaiah 1:2).

Everything God created is subject to God and his saints. All creatures have eyes, ears, and can obey when commanded. In spiritual warfare, there is nothing like living and nonliving things. Everything is alive before God. If you do not want to control the creatures, the devil and his agents will.

There is always a spirit behind any spiritual or physical organization. You can mobilize and assign, or command all heavenly resources to help you in battle. We must learn how to use everything within and around to serve us in dealing with the wicked. The house where the wicked life, the car they drive, the bed they sleep and all that is in their possession can obey you. The waters inside the bodies of the wicked and their blood can obey your command. The whole creation is earnestly waiting for the saints to address them.

'*For the earnest expectation of the creature waiteth for the manifestation of the sons of God*' (Romans 8:19).

'*And out of the ground the Lord God formed every beast of the field, and every fowl of the air; and brought them unto Adam to see what he would call them: and whatsoever Adam called every living creature, that was the name thereof. And Adam gave names to all cattle, and to the fowl of the air, and to every beast of the field; but for Adam there was not found an help meet for him*' (Genesis 2:19-20).

'*Thou shalt also decree a thing, and it shall be established unto thee: and the light shall shine upon thy ways*' (Job 22:28).

Joshua communed with God and He confirmed to Joshua that his victory over the Amorites was on a particular day. Immediately Joshua got the confirmation, he addressed the sun and the moon to suspend their movements and they obeyed. The sun heard his voice and stood still for a whole day. The moon remained in action for a whole day. The sun and the moon withdrew their services from the gods of Amorites until Joshua was satisfied with the victory.

' Then spake Joshua to the Lord in the day when the Lord delivered up the Amorites before the children of Israel, and he said in the sight of Israel, Sun, stand thou still upon Gibeon; and thou, Moon, in the valley of Ajalon. And the sun stood still, and the moon stayed, until the people had avenged themselves upon their enemies. Is not this written in the book of Jasher? So, the sun stood still in the midst of heaven, and hasted not to go down about a whole day. And there was no day like that before it or after it, that the Lord hearkened unto the voice of a man: for the Lord fought for Israel (Joshua 10:12-14).*

Nothing can stop you from ordering any creature to withdraw its service from a person, place or thing once you obtain permission from God. You are permitted to stop the wicked and all their influences in your life. The centurion at Capernaum, understood very well what being in authority meant.

'*And when Jesus was entered into Capernaum, there came unto him a centurion, beseeching him, and saying, Lord, my servant lieth at home sick of the palsy, grievously tormented. And Jesus saith unto him, I will come and heal him. The centurion answered and said, Lord, I am not worthy that thou shouldest come under my roof: but speak the word only, and my servant shall be healed. For I am a man under authority, having soldiers under me: and I say to this man, Go, and he goeth; and to another, Come, and he cometh; and to my servant, Do this, and he doeth it*' (Matthew 8:5-9).

The centurion told Jesus that he did not need his physical presence. What he needed was for Jesus to issue a word of command, which he believed every demon would obey. What you need in a time of fighting from the heavens is to issue words of authority only and things will begin to happen. Believers are people with authority, having all creatures under their dominion. The wicked and all enemies of your soul are included among creatures under your dominion. They can carry out your assignment, even assignments issued against them.

All creatures are put under you, and once you say, 'Go!' they will go, and when you say 'Come', they will come. You can tell them to do anything you want on earth and they will do it.

> '*And I say also unto thee, that thou art Peter, and upon this rock I will build my church; and the gates of hell shall not prevail against it. And I will give unto thee the keys of the kingdom of heaven: and whatsoever thou shalt bind on earth shall be bound in heaven: and whatsoever thou shalt loose on earth shall be loosed in heaven*' (Matthew 16:18-19).

You have the keys of heaven in your hands, and they are master keys. It can open and close. With these keys you do not need any other key for all other keys are subject to the keys of heaven. You can lock and unlock other keys with the keys of heaven. The kingdom of heaven rules the kingdoms of the earth. Therefore, while you are on earth binding and loosing, the heavens will be responding for you belong to heaven and not the earth.

'*Again, I say unto you, that if two of you shall agree on earth as touching anything that they shall ask, it shall be done for them of my Father which is in heaven*' (Matthew 18:19).

'*And the seventy returned again with joy, saying, Lord, even the devils are subject unto us through thy name. And he said unto them, I beheld Satan as lightning fall from heaven. Behold, I give unto you power to tread on serpents and scorpions, and over all the power of the enemy: and nothing shall by any means hurt you*' (Luke 10:17-19).

The earth and all creatures cannot disagree with your agreement with heaven for all creatures are subject of your agreement. The disciples of Jesus testified that even the demons were subjected to them when they mentioned the name of Jesus. Believers have power over the powers of the enemy and nothing can by any means hurt them. There are two major ways to pray high-level prayers.

1. Praying the prayers of authority which is giving command and

2.   Praying the prayers of decrees from the heavenlies.

These two ways are identical twins from the same source. Prayers of authority and decrees are diverse and have different ways of administration, but they emanate from the same Spirit. Though with different objectives, they accomplish the same purpose. These prayers are prayed without regarding iniquities in the heart or praying against the revealed will of God. Likewise, they cannot be prayed with unbelief.

10

Decree, Command the Morning, Day and Night

' *Write ye also for the Jews, as it liketh you, in the king's name, and seal it with the king's ring: for the writing which is written in the king's name, and sealed with the king's ring, may no man reverse. Then were the king's scribes called at that time in the third month, that is, the month Sivan, on the three and twentieth day thereof; and it was written according to all that Mordecai commanded unto the Jews, and to the lieutenants, and the deputies and rulers of the provinces which are from India unto Ethiopia, an hundred twenty and seven provinces, unto every province according to the writing thereof, and unto every people after their language, and to the Jews according to their writing, and according to their language. And he wrote in the king Ahasuerus' name, and sealed it with the king's ring, and sent letters by posts on horseback, and riders on mules, camels, and young dromedaries'* (Esther 8:8-10).

A decree is to exercise authority or giving command invested upon believers by God, to say what will stand without negotiation, compromise or prior agreement. Decrees create barriers to frustrate everything satanic and wicked people do. Evil decrees from agents of Satan can be reversed, but decrees from God and his saints cannot be reserved without God's permission. Decrees can make or unmake things, kill or give life. All creatures were created by God's decree. Believers are authorized and empowered by God to imitate Him.

'And out of the ground the Lord God formed every beast of the field, and every fowl of the air; and brought them unto Adam to see what he would call them: and whatsoever Adam called every living creature, that was the name thereof' (Genesis 2:19).

'And Joshua made them that day hewers of wood and drawers of water for the congregation, and for the altar of the Lord, even unto this day, in the place which he should choose' (Joshua 9:27).

Joshua conquered a whole nation by decree and reduced them to perpetual household servants. It is written in the book of Job that you can decree a thing and it shall be established unto you. Decree brings light on the path of the righteous. Prayers of authority and decree go hand in hand. It is either you pray prayers of authority, prayers of decree or you pray both. It is very important that you get books on prayers of decrees for better understanding. I will recommend some books on Prayers of decree.

A decree is the highest level of prayer and if you have not been decreeing, you may still be very young in the school of prayer. A person who handles decrees understands that he is operating from the third heaven. Decree wisely. Prayers of authority in this book are very important and helpful. You need to take time to pray them thoroughly one after the other. You can pray it over and over up to 12 months as God directs you. Nobody has ever prayed prayers of authority and decree and failed to get results.

Job Hast thou commanded the morning since thy days; and caused the dayspring to know his place; That it might take hold of the ends of the earth, that the wicked might be shaken out of it? (Job 38:12-13).

Job nearly missed it before God intervened and question his inability to command the morning. If you command the morning, the day will obey you and your night will not say no. If you command the morning, the day-spring will direct the things of the day and night rightly without a chance to the wicked. If believers will rise to command their mornings, days and nights, the wicked will be shaken out of this earth.

11

Spiritual Warfare Section

COMMAND THE MORNING

1. Father Lord, I command my morning to scatter every evil coalition against my destiny this morning, in the name of Jesus.

2. Blood of Jesus, speak good things into my morning, in the name of Jesus.

3. You, agents of demonic gang-up against my life this morning, be frustrated by fire, in the name of Jesus.

4. I command the whole creature to favour me this morning, in the name of Jesus.

5. Every evil thing done against me by evil coalition force this morning, die, in the name of Jesus.

6. As I start this morning, O Lord, empower me to overcome evil powers, in the name of Jesus.

7. Blood of Jesus, arise and fight for me until the last enemy of my morning is frustrated, in the name of Jesus.

8. Any power that has vowed to hinder me from starting well, fall and die, in the name of Jesus.

9. I pour the blood of Jesus into my foundation this morning, in the name of Jesus.

10. Any power assigned to hinder me this morning, die, in the name of Jesus.

11. Heavenly Father, deliver me from the grip of household wickedness, in the name of Jesus.

12. Every evil force assigned to destroy me from my ancestral altars, fall and die, in the name of Jesus.

13. Every angel of darkness assisting my household enemies, fall and die, in the name of Jesus.

14. Every evil covenant that is promoting curses in my life, break, in the name of Jesus.

15. Every evil gang-up in my place of birth that is set up against my life, scatter in shame, in the name of Jesus.

16. Blood of Jesus, speak destruction unto all my uncompromising enemies, in the name of Jesus.

17. Every enemy of my destiny, attacking me in my dreams, be exposed unto death, in the name of Jesus.

18. I cut off heads of my uncompromising enemies, in the name of Jesus.

19. Any foreign hand that has vowed to poison my life, catch fire and wither, in the name of Jesus.

20. Let the morning of my enemies refuse to break, in the name of Jesus.

21. I poison the brain of my unrepentant enemy and I command them to be wasted, in the name of Jesus.

22. Any evil pronouncement that is made against my life, be reversed by force, in the name of Jesus.

23. Great God, arise and change my situation, in the name of Jesus.

24. Blood of Jesus, flow into my life and neutralize every evil deposit by Your power, in the name of Jesus.

25. Heavenly Father, let Your words rule and reign over my life, in the name of Jesus.

26. Every witchcraft verdict in my life, backfire, in the name of Jesus.

27. Let the whole creature withdraw their supports from my unrepentant enemies, in the name of Jesus.

28. I command the air my unrepentant enemy will breathe this morning to be polluted, in the name of Jesus.

COMMAND THE DAY

1. I command evil thing in my foundation to die today, in the name of Jesus.

2. Let the glory of God begin to manifest in my foundation, in the name of Jesus.

3. You this day, take me to my place in life, in the name of Jesus.

4. Let the waters in the body of my unrepentant enemies be defiled to their confusion, in the name of Jesus.

5. Heavenly Father, arise and clear my day from every evil pollution, in the name of Jesus.

6. Darkness, take over the day of my unrepentant enemies and lead them to doom, in the name of Jesus.

7. Every bad spirit in my foundation, come out and die, in the name of Jesus.

8. Lord Jesus, appear in my case and give me an immediate solution, in the name of Jesus.

9. Every stubborn yoke that has remained in my life, break now, in the name of Jesus.

10. Any power that is assigned to prolong my bondage, die, in the name of Jesus.

11. Let God intervene and deliver me today, in the name of Jesus.

12. Heavenly Father, by Your power, move me away from destruction, in the name of Jesus.

13. Any evil power that is holding me in captive, release me today, in the name of Jesus.

14. Let the chain of environmental captivity in my life break to pieces, in the name of Jesus.

15. By the anointing that breaks every yoke, I break the yoke of bondage in my life, in the name of Jesus.

16. Every family bondage in my life, break by fire, in the name of Jesus.

17. Lord my God, arise and deliver me from every evil power, in the name of Jesus.

18. Let the movements of my unrepentant enemies, be demobilized, in the name of Jesus.

19. I climb up to the top ladder of financial breakthroughs, in the name of Jesus.

20. Every evil plantation of poverty that is in my life, wither and die by fire, in the name of Jesus.

21. Every evil covenant of financial setback, break to pieces and lose your hold, in the name of Jesus.

22. Arrows of death fired towards my financial breakthrough, backfire, in the name of Jesus.

23. Let every moment of this day turn my enemy's upside down, in the name of Jesus.

24. Father Lord, release divine finances into my life today, in the name of Jesus.

25. Father Lord, give me Your blessings that make one rich without sorrows, in the name of Jesus.

26. My promotion, wherever you are, appear now by force, in the name of Jesus.

27. You this day, expire with my unrepentant enemies, in the name of Jesus.

28. My promotion, you shall not be aborted, in the name of Jesus.

29. Lord my God, promote me beyond my equals, in the name of Jesus.

30. Heavenly Father, arise and give me an unimaginable promotion, in the name of Jesus.

COMMAND THE NIGHT

1. I stand against every satanic opposition in my life this night, in the name of Jesus.

2. Every dream of backwardness in my life, die this night, in the name of Jesus.

3. Any power from my village altar that is standing against my life, scatter this night, in the name of Jesus.

4. You the earth, frustrate my unrepentant enemies, this night, in the name of Jesus.

5. Every satanic stronghold that is standing against my advancement, I pull you down tonight, in the name of Jesus.

6. Let stumbling blocks of witchcraft be removed tonight, in the name of Jesus.

7. Let hidden curses in my life that are causing me to suffer be exposed and be disgraced tonight, in the name of Jesus.

8. Every hidden curse in my life, your time is up, die tonight, in the name of Jesus.

9. Blood of Jesus, speak destruction unto every spell in my life tonight, in the name of Jesus.

10. By the power in the name of Jesus, I cancel every evil handwriting that is against me tonight, in the name of Jesus.

11. Every stubborn curse that is placed upon my life when I was a baby, die tonight, in the name of Jesus.

12. Any covenant that I entered into with any wrong person, I break you immediately, in the name of Jesus.

13. I break and release myself from the evil effects of evil soul-ties, in the name of Jesus.

14. Every marine spirit that is manipulating of my life, be nullified tonight, in the name of Jesus.

15. Any form of evil soul-tie that is assigned to destroy me, break by force tonight, in the name of Jesus.

16. Let every known and unknown evil soul-ties in my life break by force, in the name of Jesus.

17. Father Lord, empower me supernaturally tonight, in the name of Jesus.

18. Power to confront and conquer impossibilities, possess me tonight, in the name of Jesus.

19. Dream attackers, locate my enemies this night, in the name of Jesus.

20. Heavenly Father, arise in Your supernatural power and move me forward, in the name of Jesus.

21. Every stronghold of the enemy, working against my life, be pulled down, in the name of Jesus.

22. Every wall of Jericho that is standing against my life, collapse by thunder, in the name of Jesus.

23. Let the moon and other elemental forces, attack my unrepentant enemy this night, in the name of Jesus.

24. I command every creature to withdraw their services from my unrepentant enemies, in the name of Jesus.

25. Father Lord, deliver me from sexual sins tonight, in the name of Jesus.

26. Every sexual demon that has been assigned to destroy me, be roasted by Holy Ghost Fire, in the name of Jesus.

27. I command the night to destroy my destroyers, in the name of Jesus.

28. Every serpent assigned against me tonight, die, in the name of Jesus.

29. Every bewitchment targeted at my night, be frustrated, in the name of Jesus.

30. Every plan of my enemies against me tonight, backfire, in the name of Jesus.

THANK YOU!

I'd like to use this time to thank you for purchasing my books and helping my ministry and work. Any copy of my book you buy helps to fund my ministry and family, as well as offering much-needed inspiration to keep writing. My family and I are very thankful, and we take your assistance very seriously.

You have already accomplished so much, but I would appreciate an honest review of some of my books through the link below. This is critical since reviews reflect how much an author's work is respected.

Please [click here] to leave a review on Amazon. If you're viewing from a printed version, please visit amazon.com/review/create-review?asin=B087H7R4TT to leave a review.

Please be aware that I read and value all comments and reviews. You can always post a review even though you haven't finished the book yet, and then edit your reviews later.

Thank you so much as you spare a precious moment of your time and may God bless you and meet you at the very point of your need.

You can also send me an email to hello@madueke.com if you encounter any difficulty while writing your review.

PRAYER M. MADUEKE'S BESTSELLING BOOKS

Click on any of the [Buy Now] buttons to view or purchase them on my website. If you're viewing from a printed version, please visit madueke.com and search for these books.

1. Dictionary of Demons & Complete Deliverance — [Buy Now]

2. Monitoring Spirits — [Buy Now]

3. Praying with The Blood of Jesus — [Buy Now]

4. The Power of Speaking in Tongues — [Buy Now]

5. Speaking Things into Existence by Faith — [Buy Now]

6. Discerning and Defeating the Ahab & Jezebel Spirit — [Buy Now]

7. Defeating the Python Spirit — [Buy Now]

8. 35 Special Dangerous Decrees — [Buy Now]

9. 21/40 Nights of Decrees and Your Enemies Will Surrender — [Buy Now]

10. Command the Morning, Day and Night   [**Buy Now**]

11. Evil Summon   [**Buy Now**]

12. Overcoming & Destroying the Spirit of Rejection & Hatred   [**Buy Now**]

13. Queen of Heaven: Wife of Satan   [**Buy Now**]

14. The False Prophet   [**Buy Now**]

15. Dominion Over Sickness & Disease   [**Buy Now**]

16. The Battle Plan for Destroying Foundational Witchcraft   [**Buy Now**]

17. The Queen of the Coast   [**Buy Now**]

18. Dictionary of Unmerited Favor   [**Buy Now**]

19. Prayers for Breakthrough in your Business   [**Buy Now**]

20. A Jump From Evil Altar   [**Buy Now**]

21. 100 Days Prayers to Wake Up Your Lazarus   [**Buy Now**]

22. Breaking Evil Yokes   [**Buy Now**]

23. When Evil Altars are Multiplied   [**Buy Now**]

24. The Battle Plan for Destroying
    Foundational Occultism   [Buy Now]

25. Prayers for Protection   [Buy Now]

26. Prayers for Academic Success   [Buy Now]

27. Your Dream Directory   [Buy Now]

28. Prayers for Financial Breakthrough   [Buy Now]

29. Destiny and Star Hunters   [Buy Now]

30. Prayers to Pray during Courtship   [Buy Now]

31. 91 Days Decrees to Takeover the Year   [Buy Now]

32. Alone with God   [Buy Now]

33. Prayers against Satanic Oppression   [Buy Now]

34. Foundations Exposed   [Buy Now]

35. Prayers for Deliverance   [Buy Now]

36. Prayers to Heal Broken Relationship   [Buy Now]

37. Prayers for Good Health   [Buy Now]

4 Free Ebooks

In order to say a 'Thank You' for purchasing *Command the Morning, Day and Night*, I offer these books to you in appreciation. Click or type **madueke.com/free-gift** in your browser.

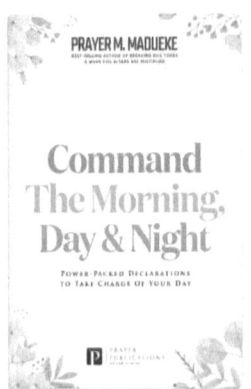

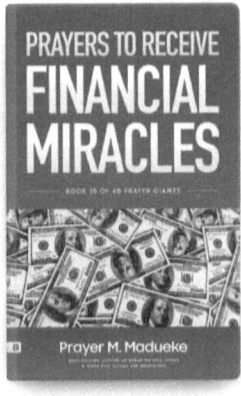

Video Bonus

I've created exclusive video content to complement the topics covered in the book. These videos provide deeper insights and discussions on the things discussed in this book, offering you a more immersive learning experience.

To access the video bonus for this course, simply click or type links.madueke.com/18CMDN in your browser.

Message from the Author

I want to see you succeed, grow, and break free from negativity and obstacles. My hope is for you to thrive, unaffected by negative influences and challenging situations. Because of that, please permit me to introduce two courses that I believe passionately will help you:

1. To break the evil altars and powers of your father's house, The role of altars in the realm of existence is very key because altars are meeting places between the physical and the spiritual, between the visible and the invisible.

   Unless a man cuts off the evil flow from the power of his father's house, he will not fulfil his destiny. Click here to learn more about my course on how to tear down unholy altars and close the enemy's entryways into your life!

2. To help you seamlessly break iron-like problems, illness, delayed marriage, poverty, or any long-standing battle.

   Discover the transformative power of Christian fasting and prayer. Remember, Matthew 17:21 teaches us, *"But this kind of demon does not go out except by prayer and fasting."* Ready to overcome your struggles? Click here to learn more about this course.

Embrace the journey ahead with faith, for through prayer, fasting, and the dismantling of evil altars, you shall unlock the doors to spiritual liberation and divine breakthrough. May your path be illuminated by His grace as you walk towards a life free from bondage.

If you're seeing this from the physical copy, type the link: madueke.com/courses in your browser to view all the courses on my website.

Prayer Madueke
CHRISTIAN AUTHOR

Christian Counselling

We were created for a greater purpose than only survival and God wants us to live a full life.

If you need prayer or counselling, or if you have any other inquiries, please visit the counselling page on my website to know when I will be available for a phone call.

Click or type **links.madueke.com/counselling** in your browser.

Let's Connect on Youtube ▶

Join me on my YouTube channel, "Prayer M. Madueke," where I share powerful insights, guidance, and prayers for spiritual breakthroughs.

Subscribe today to unlock the secrets of the Kingdom and embrace an abundant life. Let's grow together!

Click or type links.madueke.com/youtube in your browser.

An Invitation to Become a Ministry Partner

I appreciate the support and inquiries I have received regarding collaboration with my ministry. Your prayers and dedication to the work of the Kingdom are highly valued.

You can also visit the donation page on my website if you would like to contribute or learn more about supporting my ministry: madueke.com/donate.

Thank you for your continued support and faithfulness in Christ Jesus.